Swahili Learners' Reference Grammar

Swahili Learners' Reference Grammar

By

Katrina Daly Thompson

Antonia Folárìn Schleicher

Foreword by
John Mugane

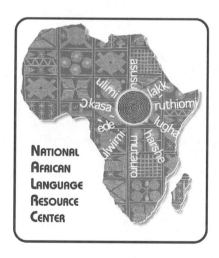

NATIONAL
AFRICAN
LANGUAGE
RESOURCE
CENTER

NALRC Press

African Language Learners' Reference Grammar Series
Antonia Folárin Schleicher, Series General Editor

The development of the NALRC African Language Learners' Reference Grammar Series is made possible through a grant from the U.S. Department of Education.

NALRC Publications Office
Kristi Hobson, Editor
Karin Gleisner, Assistant Editor
Amadou Fofana, Assistant Editor
Mary Rohrdanz & Janet Trembley, Graphic Designers
Aiming Wang, Financial Manager

NALRC African Language Learners' Reference Grammar Series

Library of Congress Cataloging-in-Publication Data

Thompson, Katrina Daly, 1975-
  Swahili learners' reference grammar/Katrina Daly Thompson, Antonia
  Folárin Schleicher; forward by John Mugane.
  p. cm. -- (African language learners' reference grammar series; 1)
  Includes bibliographical references and index
  ISBN 1-58684-115-7 (alk. paper)
  1. Swahili language--Grammar. 2. Swahili language--Textbooks for
foreign speakers--English. I. Schleicher, Antonia Yétúndé Folárin, 1953-
II. Title. III. Series
PL8702 .T48 2001
496'.39282421—dc21

African Language Learners' Reference Grammar Series

The *African Language Learners' Reference Grammar Series* is written for speakers of English who are learning African languages. Since many language learners are not familiar with grammatical terminology used in their textbooks, the books in this series seek to explain the basic terminology and concepts of English grammar that are necessary for understanding the grammar of an African language. The primary objective of the *African Language Learners' Reference Grammar* Series is to provide language learners with grammar books that will supplement their textbooks. These books are not intended to replace a textbook. The books in the series assume no formal knowledge of English grammar and are written in easy to understand language.

Interested parties may contact the National African Language Resource Center (NALRC) about the possibility of working with the Center to publish a similar grammar book for their respective languages. Manuscripts are subject to external review and must follow the theoretical framework established for the series.

A series such as this depends on the vision, good will and labor of many. Special appreciation is extended to the U.S. Department of Education's IEGPS (International and Education and Graduate Programs Service), the NALRC staff members, the NALRC's Field Advisory, National Advisory, and Local Advisory Boards, and the University of Wisconsin-Madison College of Letters and Science, especially Jane Tylus (Associate Dean for the Arts and Humanities) and Phillip Certain (Dean of the College of Letters and Science), as well as various individuals who support the efforts of the

NALRC. Without the support, advice and assistance of all, the *African Language Learners' Reference Grammar Series* would not have become a reality.

Antonia Folárìn Schleicher
Series General Editor

FOREWORD

This monograph is a pedagogical grammar of Swahili that is well illustrated and exhaustive both in the wide range of phenomena considered and examples provided. The book provides the grammar of Swahili in such a way that the novice and the advanced student will constantly find recourse to read and revisit the contents of the book at various points of their study.

The oft remarked elegance of the Swahili language will be appreciated even by those whose need is not to speak Swahili but merely to understand the workings of its grammar components. Crucial notions concerning nouns, verbs and adjectives and the way these categories relate to one another are clearly laid out so that no knowledge of linguistics and teaching methodology is assumed or expected. The book is organized in a way that makes it good for both quick and detailed referencing. It follows the fundamentals of good pedagogical grammars in that it is written with careful attention to detail matched with simplicity of explanation. The end result is that the learner will now be equipped with the fundamentals of how the Swahili language is constituted. Grammar remains an important component in second language learning in spite of much commentary to the contrary. This grammar, being a work of considerable quality, supports a teaching philosophy that places a premium on learner autonomy. Instead of students relying on teachers, teachers evolve to become facilitators and mentors of the learning process. This book will particularly aid our diverse teaching personnel who may be presently apprehensive about teaching grammar or integrating it into their lesson plans.

This grammar, being the inaugural volume in the *African Language Learners' Reference Grammar Series*, is sure to serve as a model for the upcoming ones. The first of its kind for

Swahili, this book should be a delight to those of us who champion the nurturing of learner engagement and learner initiative as some of the necessary elements towards lifelong learning. This book is a milestone for the field of African language learning and teaching and will hopefully be met with the applause it deserves. The book *Swahili Learners' Reference Grammar* is testament to the excellent work being accomplished by the National African Language Resource Center (NALRC) at the University of Wisconsin-Madison. The field owes many thanks to the authors and to the NALRC.

John Mugane
President-Elect, African Language Teachers Association (ALTA)
Assistant Professor of Linguistics
Ohio University, Athens, Ohio
January 2001

ABOUT THE AUTHORS

Antonia Yétúndé Folárìn Schleicher is a Professor of African Languages and Linguistics at the University of Wisconsin-Madison. She is also the Director of National African Language Resource Center (NALRC), funded by the Department of Education. She currently teaches courses such as Yoruba language and culture, African linguistics, second language acquisition, with specific reference to African languages, and a culture course on Yoruba life and civilization. She is experienced in developing both textual and technology materials for learning African languages. She is the author of three textbooks and two CD-ROMs for teaching and learning Yoruba. These textbooks and CD-ROMs are now used as models for developing other Less Commonly Taught Language (LCTL) materials. She has also co-authored a book with Professor Lioba Moshi, titled "African Language Pedagogy: An Emerging Field." She is currently co-authoring a book on "Guidelines for Developing African Language Textbooks." Professor Schleicher has organized different national workshops on how to develop materials for African languages and LCTLs in general. She is familiar with how different language acquisition theories can impact the development of textbooks for learning and teaching languages.

She is the Immediate Past-President of the African Language Teachers Association (ALTA), the President-Elect of the National Council of Organizations of Less Commonly Taught Languages (NCOLCTL), and an Executive Board Member of the UW-Madison Teaching Academy.

Katrina Daly Thompson is a doctoral student in the Department of African Languages and Literature at the UW-Madison. A student of both Shona and Swahili, she completed her M.A. degree in 1999 with a thesis entitled

"The Translator as Trickster: How *A Grain of Wheat* becomes *Tsanga Yembeu*." In 1999 she spent seven weeks in Tanzania studying advanced Swahili as a fellow on the Fulbright Hayes Group Project Abroad, and in 2001 she will spend nine months doing research in Zimbabwe. Her research and teaching interests include Shona and Swahili languages and cultures, African popular cultures, post-colonial literatures and translation theory and practice. Katrina spent July 2000 studying technology and language teaching at Middlebury College with a grant from the Mellon Foundation. She is currently working on a dissertation on Shona film and television.

TABLE OF CONTENTS

Preface 5
To the Learners 7
Acknowledgements 11
INTRODUCTION 13
  Parts of speech
  Meaning
  Function

NOUNS

Chapter 1	Introduction to Nouns	19
Chapter 2	Articles	25
Chapter 3	Noun class	29
Chapter 4	Verbal nouns	45
	Present infinitives	
	Perfect infinitives	
	Gerund	
Chapter 5	Negative verbal nouns	53

PRONOUNS

Chapter 6	Introduction to Pronouns	59
Chapter 7	Personal pronouns	63
Chapter 8	Reflexive pronouns	67
Chapter 9	Interrogative pronouns	71
Chapter 10	Demonstrative pronouns	81
Chapter 11	Possessive pronouns	89
Chapter 12	Relative pronouns/constructions	93
	Infixed relatives	
	Tenseless relatives	
Chapter 13	Indefinite pronouns	105

ADJECTIVES

Chapter 14	Introduction to Adjectives	113
	Descriptive adjectives	115
	Attributive adjectives	
	Predicate adjectives	

Chapter 16   Possessive adjectives   121
                          Possessor
                          Possessed
                          Reflexive possessives
                          Non-reflexive possessives
                          Possessive contractions
Chapter 17   Interrogative adjectives   131
Chapter 18   Demonstrative adjectives   135
Chapter 19   Subjects   145
Chapter 20   Subject prefixes   149

VERBS

Chapter 21   Introduction   to   Verbs   and   Verb
                  Tenses   161
                          Transitive and intransitive
                          verbs
                          Agglutination
Chapter 22   Present   167
                          The -na- tense
                          The –a- tense
Chapter 23   Negative present   177
Chapter 24   Past   181
Chapter 25   Negative past   187
Chapter 26   Perfect   191
Chapter 27   Negative perfect   195
Chapter 28   Future   199
Chapter 29   Negative future   203
Chapter 30   The verb 'to be'   207
Chapter 31   The locative verb 'to be'   219
Chapter 32   The verb 'to have'   225
Chapter 33   Auxiliary verbs   237

Chapter 34   Objects   243
                          Object markers
Chapter 35   Direct objects   249
Chapter 36   Indirect objects   255

Chapter 37   Introduction to Mood   259
              The indicative mood
Chapter 38   The imperative mood   263
Chapter 39   The subjunctive mood   267
Chapter 40   The conditional mood   277
Chapter 41   Verb extensions   279
              Root verbs
              Applied/prepositional
              Stative extensions
              Causative extensions
              Reversive extensions
              Passive extensions
              Reciprocal extensions
Chapter 42   Participles   289
Chapter 43   Compound tenses   295
Chapter 44   Active & passive voice   303
              Active verbs
              Passive verb
              Agent

ADVERBS

Chapter 45   Adverbs   311

CONJUNCTIONS

Chapter 46   Conjunctions   319

PREPOSITIONS

Chapter 47   Prepositions & prepositional phrases   327
Chapter 48   Object of the preposition   335

SENTENCES

Chapter 49   Sentences, phrases & clauses . .   341
Chapter 50   Declarative & interrogative sentences   359
Chapter 51   Conditional sentences   365
Chapter 52   Direct & indirect statements   371
Chapter 53   Comparisons   375

MISCELLANEOUS

Chapter 54	Reduplication	385
Chapter 55	Interjections	389
	Glossary	393
	Index	403
	Answer Key	415

PREFACE

The *Swahili Learners' Reference Grammar* is written for speakers of English who are learning Swahili. Since many language learners are not familiar with grammatical terminology used in their textbooks, this book explains the basic terminology and concepts of English grammar that are necessary for understanding the grammar of Swahili. It assumes no formal knowledge of English grammar and is written in very simple language.

The primary objective of the *Swahili Learners' Reference Grammar* is to provide Swahili learners with a grammar book that will supplement their textbooks. It is not intended to replace a Swahili textbook. Occasionally, learners need more extensive explanations of the structures presented in their textbooks. This manual provides such additional detail. The grammar is arranged by topic to help learners locate information easily. For example, information on nouns can be found in Chapters 1-5.

The following are the design features of the *Swahili Learners' Reference Grammar:*

1. The organizational design is built around the basic word order of a Swahili sentence. The bulk of the manual focuses on nouns, pronouns, adjectives, verbs, adverbs, and objects. The text also includes various types of work with compound and complex sentences and with several other topics.

2. The grammar book presents the underlying structure of Swahili in a coherent and orderly manner.

3. The resources in this manual are built on a framework of explanations, examples, and short reviews. Each chapter is a self-contained discussion of a particular grammar topic. A

brief definition of the grammar topic is followed by an explanation and examples of the way the grammatical construction is used in English. Then a parallel section illustrates the use of the same grammar point in Swahili, step by step, using sample sentences translated from Swahili into English.

4. It is assumed that the study of grammar should be tied to the real needs of learners both to help them better understand course materials and to expand their accuracy and fluency in Swahili.

5. The presentation of individual grammar items is tied to the larger context of the basic structure of Swahili. For example, the meanings of individual tenses are presented within the framework of the verb system.

6. The materials in this manual include the study of processes as well as particular grammatical items. For example, compounding, as well as the present tense particle, are covered in the section on VERBS.

TO THE LEARNERS

The *Swahili Learners' Reference Grammar* is written to help you understand the basic grammatical terms that you may not be familiar with in your Swahili textbook. It is hoped that this manual will not only help you to acquire grammatical competency in Swahili, but also in English. Knowing the grammar of any language you are learning is very important because it allows you to express your thoughts and intentions in a way that is acceptable to native speakers. Many times, grammar mistakes can make your speaking and writing difficult to understand. In Swahili, an example in which grammar affects meaning directly is if you use a past tense marker "**li**" instead of a future tense marker "**ta**" when describing to a friend your plans for the future.

The table of contents and the index are provided to help you to locate the grammatical terms and concepts that you want to understand in greater detail. Remember to use both the TABLE OF CONTENTS and the INDEX on a regular basis.

Make sure you understand the explanations and the examples provided both in English and in Swahili. Whenever a REVIEW is provided, remember to do it to assess your knowledge of the grammatical terms you are learning. If your answers do not match the ANSWER KEY, make sure you review the section before you move on to another section.

Below are some strategies that can help you to learn the grammar of Swahili in a more effective manner:

1. **Be on the lookout for patterns**: Don't wait for your instructor or others to point out a pattern; look for it yourself. Sometimes the patterns that you can recognize yourself will be more helpful than those given in your textbook or presented in this manual, because they are

organized in ways that are clearer to you. If you uncover the patterns yourself, it will be easier to remember and follow them.

2. **Learn the rules**: Make sure you understand how a particular rule works. This will reduce the amount of memorization you will need to do.

3. **Organize**: After you have constructed your own grammar tables in the way that makes the most sense to you, make sure you review them and add any new information that you acquire. For example, you can make a table of Swahili noun classes, tenses, or negative tenses. Each time you learn a new word that belongs to a particular category you have set up, enter it in your table. This is especially important if the word is an exception to a rule and needs special attention.

4. **Experiment**: Try to experiment with rules because most grammar rules have boundaries that you need to discover by yourself to avoid mistakes. The way to find the boundaries is to keep applying a rule until you discover that it no longer works. For example, in Swahili you cannot always apply agreement rules simply according to what class a word is in:

kitabu/vitabu (class 7/8):   **Kitabu kinapotea.**
                                        Vitabu vinapotea.

kiongozi/viongozi (class 7/8):   **Kiongozi anaenda.**
                                        Viongozi wanae
                                        (use class ½ agreements)

5. **Work towards mastery when doing grammar exercises**: When doing oral grammar exercises in class, at home, or in the language lab, carefully focus on the grammar. At this point, every one of the teacher's corrections or the correct responses on tape should be accurately repeated. Many learners habitually listen passively to the teacher's corrections or the models on tape without repeating the correct form. Avoid falling into this bad habit, as it is only by repeating the corrected version that you give yourself an opportunity to learn it. When working on a grammar point, strive to be 100% correct. In this way, when your attention is diverted to other considerations, you will be more likely to recall the correct form.

6. **Avoid repeated errors**: Try to understand why you consistently make a certain kind of error. Is it because you are not clear about the rule? Or is it that you have totally misunderstood the rule? Or could it be that you have not learned the rule boundaries – that is, its exceptions? You can avoid making the same mistake by checking your textbook, this manual, or by asking your teacher for an explanation or clarification.

7. **Note whether additional work has any effect on your performance**: Sometimes extra practice – such as doing grammar drills – may not improve your speaking accuracy. However, using language in real-life situations may be very beneficial. The amount of time spent on an activity may not be as important as finding and using the type of activity that helps your learning.

8. **Be patient**: There is no language that is grammar-free, although some languages have more complex grammatical systems than others. It is impossible to learn, much less remember, all the rules in a limited period of time. It will take some time before you will be able to speak and write

without grammatical errors.   Work on your grammar diligently but patiently. Learning one rule at a time, practicing often and doing frequent reviews are good learning principles.

ACKNOWLEDGMENTS

We would like to acknowledge our appreciation for the support of the National African Language Resource Center (NALRC) through funds from the Department of Education, Grant # P229A990001, which provided the financial support for the preparation of this book. Without such support, this book would not have been possible. Our grateful appreciation is also extended to the following people who have contributed one way or the other towards making this project possible: Magdalena Hauner, Anne Lewinson, Zeynab Shaaban, Himid Ali, Abdul-swammad Ali, Ammar Ali, Assim Ali, Hud Ali, and Hilda Kokuhirwa.

We are greatly indebted to all the Swahili language scholars, such as Alwiya Omar, John Inniss, John Mugane, and F.E.M.K. Senkoro, who took time out from their busy schedules to review, in various stages of development, some or all the chapters of this book and provided valuable suggestions that helped in shaping the final draft of this book. We, however, assume full responsibility for any errors in this book.

Words are inadequate to express our thanks to Kristi Hobson and Karin Gleisner, who served as editor and assistant editor for this project. Both Kristi and Karin spent a great deal of time, not only making sure that some of the Swahili examples were accurate but also assisting with the overall organization of the book. Our thanks also go to Amadou Fofana, who helped to read through the first draft to be sure that it followed the intended organizational structure.

This book is dedicated to Charles, Carla, Anthony and the UW–Madison Fall 2000 Swahili students.

INTRODUCTION

Learning Swahili, like learning any foreign language, requires that you look at each word in terms of its part of speech, its meanings, and its function. This book is designed to help you understand the **part of speech,** the **meaning** and the **function** of the Swahili forms that you will be learning.

1. Part of speech

Words are grouped by types and each type is called a part of speech. Here is a list of the nine different parts of speech used in English:

Noun	Article
Pronoun	Conjunction
Verb	Preposition
Adverb	Interjection
Adjective	

Each part of speech has its own rules. You must learn to identify the part of speech for each word so that you will know which rules to apply. Understanding the rules for each part of speech will help you understand the function and relationship of the words in both English and Swahili sentences.

Look at how the word *love* functions in the sentences that follow:

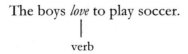

The boys *love* to play soccer.
|
verb

My *love* for you is great.
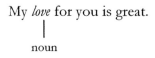

noun

Charles wrote Rosa a *love* letter.
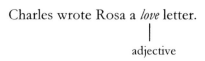

adjective

The English word *love* is the same in all three sentences, but in Swahili different words will be used for the verb, the noun and the adjective.

2. Meaning

An English word must be connected with a Swahili word that has an equivalent meaning. For example, the word *water*, in English, has the same basic meaning as the Swahili word **maji**.

The best way to learn words with equivalent meanings is to memorize the words. However, there are some English words that are borrowed into Swahili. These kinds of words are easier to learn because they are very close to the English counterparts. Some examples include:

ENGLISH	SWAHILI
motorcar	**motokaa**
America	**Amerika**
office	**ofisi**
soccer	**soka**

Sometimes, if you know one Swahili word it can help you to learn another. For example knowing that the Swahili word **kiti** means *chair* should help you to learn that **mwenyekiti** means *chairperson*. Similarly, knowing that **kuzungumza** means *to converse* will help you to learn that **mazungumzo** means *conversation*.

For the most part, there is little or no similarity between words, and knowing one Swahili word will not help you learn another. As a general rule, such words must be memorized separately. For example, knowing that **bibi** means *grandmother* will not help you to learn that **babu** is *grandfather*.

In addition, there are some combinations of words that take on a special meaning. Such words are referred to as **idioms**. Idioms are usually unique to each language. For example, in Swahili, **kuenda** means *to go*, while **wazimu** means *spirits*. However, **kuenda wazimu** means *to go crazy*. You need to pay special attention to these kinds of idiomatic expressions so that you can use them appropriately.

3. Function

A word must be identified according to the function it performs in the sentence. Each word, whether in English or in Swahili, serves a unique function in the sentence. Determining this function will help you to find the proper Swahili equivalent.

Look at how the word *her* functions in the sentences that follow:

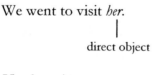

We went to visit *her*.
|
direct object

Her dress is new.
|
adjective

In English the word *her* is the same in both sentences, but in Swahili two different words, each following a different set of rules, must be used because the word *her* has two different functions.

While studying Swahili, you must learn to recognize the part of speech, the meaning, and the function of each word within a sentence.

TAKE NOTE

Since you already know English, this book will show you how to identify parts of speech in English. You will then learn to compare and contrast English and Swahili constructions. This will give you a better understanding of the explanations you receive in class or find in your Swahili textbook.

NOUNS

Chapter 1
INTRODUCTION TO NOUNS

A **noun** is a word that signifies a person, animal, place, thing, event or idea. For example:

•	a person	*teacher, student, nurse, doctor, grandmother, Mr., Sheriff*
•	an animal	*dog, cow, bull, lion, bird, hyena, elephant*
•	a place	*house, school, city, state, country, continent, island, Tanzania, Kenya, Mecca*
•	a thing	*book, shirt, computer, drum, veil, dish, food*
•	an event or activity	*birth, death, marriage, graduation, soccer, sleep, the Olympics*
•	an idea or concept	*freedom, wealth, love, power, beauty, history, Organization of African Unity*

As you can see, a noun can name something tangible (i.e. that you can touch), such as *glass, coffee,* and *grandmother,* or it can name something abstract, such as *racism, music,* and *courage.*

There are two types of nouns, **common** and **proper**. A noun that refers to any person, animal, place, thing, event or idea that is not specific is called a **common noun**. A common noun never begins with a capital letter unless it is the first word in a sentence. All the words above that begin with a lower-case letter are common nouns. A noun that names a particular place, animal, place, thing, event or idea is a **proper noun**. A proper noun is always capitalized. All the capitalized words above are examples of proper nouns.

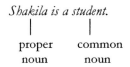

A noun that is made up of two words is a **compound noun**. A compound noun can be made of two common nouns, such as *trade unions* and *mother tongue*, or two proper nouns, such as *East Africa*.

IN ENGLISH
To train yourself to recognize nouns, read the following paragraph where the nouns are in italics.

Swahili is spoken extensively in *Tanzania, Kenya* and *Uganda*. Along the *coast* of *Kenya* and *Tanzania*, and on the *islands* near their *coasts*, it is the first *language* of many *people*. *Others* speak it as a second *language*, not only in these three *countries* but also in the *Democratic Republic of the Congo, Zambia, Malawi, Mozambique*, and even *Saudi Arabia*.

KWA KISWAHILI

A noun is called **jina** or **nomino**. The plural, *nouns*, are **majina** or **nomino**. Swahili nouns are identified in the same way as they are in English; that is, they can signify people, animals, places, things, events or ideas. Study the following examples:

- a person
fundi (*craftsperson*), **askari** (*soldier*), **kipofu** (*blind person*), **Mkristo** (*Christian*), **Profesa Senkoro** (*Professor Senkoro*)

- an animal
chui (*leopard*), **swala** (*antelope*), **kobe** (*turtle*), **mbu** (*mosquito*), **panya** (*rat*)

- a place
chuo kikuu (*university*), **msikiti** (*mosque*), **shamba** (*field*), **eneo** (*space*), **Unguja** (*Zanzibar*), **Msumbiji** (*Mozambique*)

- a thing
pipi (*candy*), **zawadi** (*gift*), **kitambaa** (*cloth*), **kalamu** (*pen*), **mkono** (*hand*)

- an event or activity
arusi (*wedding*), **sherehe** (*party*), **kushona** (*sewing*), **mchezo** (*game*), **safari** (*journey*)

- an idea or concept
falsafa (*philosophy*), **hesabu** (*math*), **ushirika** (*cooperation*), **elimu** (*education*), **uhuru** (*revolution*)

A common noun is called **nomino ya jumla** or **nomino ya jamii** and a proper noun is **nomino kamili** or **nomino ya pekee.** A compound noun is called **nomino ambatani.**

Shakila ni mwanafunzi.
Shakila is (a) student.

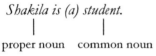

proper noun   common noun

To train yourself to recognize nouns, read the following paragraph (followed by its English translation) where nouns are in italics.

Taasisi ya *Kiswahili* na *Lugha* za Kigeni iko katika *kisiwa* cha *Unguja, mji* wa *Zanzibar. Zanzibar* ina *watu* wengi wa *asili* mbalimbali: *Waafrika, Waarabu, Wahindi, Wachina,* na *wengine. Wageni* wengi wanasafiri *Zanzibar* kusoma hapo *Taasisini.* Wanaweza kusoma *Kiswahili, Kiarabu,* na *lugha* nyingine za Kiafrika na za *dunia.* Ni *shule* nzuri sana.

(The *Institute* of *Swahili* and Foreign *Languages* is on the *island* of *Zanzibar,* in the city of *Zanzibar. Zanzibar* has many *people* of various *backgrounds: Africans, Arabs, Indians, Chinese* and others. Many *foreigners* travel to Zanzibar to study at the *Institute. They* can study *Swahili, Arabic,* and other African and *world languages. It* is a very good *school.*)

TERMS USED TO TALK ABOUT NOUNS

- **NUMBER** – A noun has a number. It can be classified as singular or plural.
- **GENDER/CLASS** – Every Swahili noun is associated with one of eighteen classes. English nouns have only three classes, usually known as gender; the classes are masculine, feminine and neuter. Swahili nouns do not differentiate in terms of masculine, feminine and neuter genders.
- **COUNT** OR **NON-COUNT** – A noun can be classified as to whether it is a count or non-count noun; that is, whether it refers to something that can be counted or not.
- **FUNCTION** – A noun can have two different functions in a sentence; that is, it can be the subject of the sentence or an object.

REVIEW

Circle the nouns in the following sentences.

1. I marked the date of the party on the calendar.

2. Lulu broke her leg while riding her bicycle to Dodoma.

3. The film we saw yesterday disturbed me.

4. A woman's beauty is her personality, not her appearance.

5. Dar es Salaam is a city the President has always wanted to visit.

Chapter 2
ARTICLES

An **article** is a word placed before a noun to show whether the noun refers to a specific person, animal, place, thing, event or idea, or to a nonspecific person, animal, place, thing, event or idea.

a specific piece of cloth
|
She wrapped *the* piece of cloth around her shoulders.

She wrapped *a* piece of cloth around her head.
|
a nonspecific piece of cloth

IN ENGLISH
There are two types of articles, **definite articles** and **indefinite articles**. A **definite article** is used before a noun referring to a specific person, place, animal, thing or idea. There is one definite article, *the*.

He stole *the* books from me.
|
some specific books

An **indefinite article** is used before a noun referring to a non-specific person, animal, place, thing, event or idea. There are two indefinite articles, *a* and *an*. *A* is used when the noun it precedes begins with a consonant.

I bought *a* dress.
|
not a specific dress

An is used when the noun it precedes begins with a vowel (*a, e, i, o,* or *u*).

> Zuhura peeled *an* orange.
> |
> not a specific orange

Plural nouns that do not refer to someone or something specific are used without an article.

> Kezilahabi writes *novels.*
> |
> not specific novels

KWA KISWAHILI

The grammatical term for articles is **vibainishi,** but there are no articles in Swahili. When you translate a sentence into English, articles, if appropriate, must be added. Your knowledge of English and the meaning of the sentence will help you to add the article which best fits the sentence's meaning. For example, the following Swahili sentences can each be translated in two ways:

> **Mtoto ataenda shuleni.**
> *A child will go to school.*
> *The child will go to school.*

> **Watoto wataenda shuleni.**
> *Children will go to school.*
> *The children will go to school.*

Even though there are no articles in Swahili, you need to be aware of their use in English. Sometimes you will use demonstrative adjectives to approximate the function of articles. For example:

Watoto <u>hawa</u> wataenda shuleni.
<u>These</u> children will go to school.

You will learn more about demonstrative adjectives in Chapter 18.

REVIEW

Using the word for word translations of Swahili sentences into English, write complete English sentences. You will need to add the appropriate articles.

1. **Mwanafunzi alisoma kitabu.**
    student   read   book

    _____

2. **Mwandishi anakaa huko bara.**
    writer   lives   (there on) mainland

    _____

3. **Mtoto atakula chungwa na mkate.**
    child   will eat   orange   and   bread
    _____

CHAPTER 3
NOUN CLASS

A **noun class** is a set of nouns in a language that shows the same patterns of word or a set of nouns that shows the same system of agreements between different parts of speech.

Swahili, like any other Bantu language, has a well- defined noun class system. Swahili nouns can be classified as Class 1, 2, 3, 4, 5, 6, 7, 8, 9, 10, 11, 14, 15, 16, 17, or 18. Class 12 is extremely rare in Swahili, and Class 13 does not exist. Below is an example of a Swahili sentence that illustrates how the class system works.

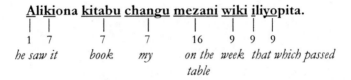

(He saw my book on the table last week.)

Number in the grammatical sense means that a word can be classified as singular or plural. When a noun refers to one person, animal, thing, place, or event, it is called **singular.** When it refers to more than one, it is called **plural.**

More parts of speech indicate number in Swahili than in English and there are more spelling and pronunciation changes in Swahili than in English.

ENGLISH	**SWAHILI**
nouns	*nouns* **nomino/majina**
verbs	*verbs* **vitenzi**
pronouns	*pronouns* **viwakilishi nomino**
	adjectives **vivumishi**
	relative constructions **virejeshi**

Since each part of speech follows its own rules to indicate number, you will find number discussed in the chapters on relative constructions, adjectives, pronouns, and verbs. This chapter will only explain the number of nouns.

IN ENGLISH

English is usually not regarded as a class language, but there are some examples in English that can illustrate how nouns in different classes behave. For example, consider pluralization in English:

SINGULAR	PLURAL
cat	cats
house	houses
dress	dresses
farmer	farmers
pencil	pencils
church	churches

All these nouns form their plural the same way, by adding *s* or *es*. Therefore, these nouns and others like them can be said to be in the same noun class. Now consider these words:

sheep	sheep
deer	deer

These do not change in the plural. They belong to another noun class. Other examples are:

mouse	mice
louse	lice
goose	geese
foot	feet
tooth	teeth
man	men

The above examples form yet another noun class, one that changes the vowel "inside" the noun to make it plural.

Notice that these noun classes in English are no longer called noun classes. They are called **"regular"** and **"irregular"** nouns. All the nouns that take 's' are called regular nouns, while those that do not take s are called irregular nouns. This is because, in English, only the 's' plural class can have new words added to it. When a class can get new words, it is called "productive". In English plural formation, there are many noun classes, but only one is productive (hence they are called "regular", while other noun classes are not productive, hence they are called "irregular").

Some nouns, called **collective nouns,** refer to a group of persons or things, but the noun itself is considered singular.

The soccer *team* is doing well this season.
The *family* is moving to Iringa.
The *committee* has a difficult decision to make.

KWA KISWAHILI

The word for grammatical number is **namba.** When used to refer to nouns it is called **namba ya jina.** A singular noun is called **jina la umoja** and a plural noun is **jina la wingi.** As in English, the plural form of a Swahili noun is usually spelled differently than the singular. Every noun belongs to a **noun class,** and each class of nouns has its own rules for forming the singular and the plural. There are sixteen classes (1-11 and 14-18). For most noun classes (1-11), the odd numbers denote the singular and the even numbers denote the plural.

CLASS	SINGULAR	PLURAL	CLASS
1	**mtu** (*person*)	**watu** (*people*)	2
3	**mti** (*tree*)	**miti** (*trees*)	4
5	**jengo** (*building*)	**majengo** (*buildings*)	6
7	**kitabu** (*book*)	**vitabu** (*books*)	8
9	**ndege** (*plane*)	**ndege** (*planes*)	10
11	**usiku** (*night*)	**siku** (*nights*)	10

You can see that each class has a system for forming the plural. You should also note that class 12 is not listed because it is infrequently used and has no regular plural form.

In Swahili, all noun classes are productive, just as in any Noun Class language. Swahili nouns follow rules for grammatical class. The word for class or classes is **ngeli**.[1] A few generalizations can be made about the kinds of nouns that fall into each of the noun classes. However, there are many exceptions, so you should always memorize the class of each noun in both the singular and plural.

CLASS 1 ngeli ya kwanza

Nouns in class 1 are singular, and refer to living things such as people and animals. They usually begin with the **nominal prefix m-**, but sometimes begin with **mw-** or, rarely, with **mu-**. In Swahili a nominal prefix is called **kiambishi awali cha jina**.

> **mtu** (*person*)
> **mwalimu** (*teacher*)
> **muumba** (*creator*)

Some singular nouns do not belong to class 1, but, because they refer to people and animals, use class 1 agreements in most grammatical contexts.

> **kijana** (*young person*, class 7)
> **kipofu** (*blind person*, class 7)
> **paka** (*cat*, class 9)

You will learn more about how to use class 1 agreements in Chapters 20 (Subject Prefixes) and 34 (Objects), and in the series of chapters on adjectives and pronouns (6-20).

Proper nouns that refer to people are also treated as if they were in class 1. Because many Swahili names are words that

---

[1] The word **namna** (*type or kind*) is also used for grammatical class. See G.W. Broomfield, *Sarufi ya Kiswahili* (London: Sheldon Press, 1931): 40-47.

are also used as common nouns, you might confuse them with the noun of another class. To avoid this mistake, take note if the noun is capitalized, which will indicate that it is a proper noun.

COMMON NOUNS	PROPER NOUNS
juma (*week*, class 5)	**Juma** (*a boy's name*, class 1)
zawadi (*gift*, class 9)	**Zawadi** (*a girl's name*, class 1)
sudi (*luck*, class 9)	**Sudi** (*a boy's name*, class 1)

CLASS 2 ngeli ya pili
Nouns in class 2 are plural of nouns in class 1, and they refer to living things such as people and animals. They always begin with the nominal prefix **wa-**.

> **watu** (*people*)
> **walimu** (*teachers*)
> **waumba** (*creators*)

Some singular nouns do not belong to class 2, but because they refer to people and animals, they use class 2 agreements in most grammatical contexts.

> **vijana** (*young people*, class 8)
> **vipofu** (*blind people*, class 8)
> **paka** (*cats*, class 10)

You will learn more about how to use class 2 agreements in Chapters 20 (Subject Prefixes) and 34 (Objects), and in the series of chapters on adjectives and pronouns (6-20)

CLASS 3 ngeli ya tatu

Nouns in class 3 are singular. They begin with the nominal prefix **m**-. Almost all singular nouns that refer to plants are in class 3, but many other objects are as well.

mti *(tree)* **mgomba** *(banana tree)*
mzizi *(root)* **mradi** *(project)*
mkutano *(meeting)*

CLASS 4 ngeli ya nne

Nouns in class 4 are the plural of nouns in class 3 and they begin with the nominal prefix **mi**-. Almost all plural nouns that refer to plants are in class 4, but many other objects are as well.

miti *(trees)* **migomba** *(banana trees)*
miradi *(projects)*

CLASS 5 ngeli ya tano

Nouns in class 5 are singular, and usually refer to inanimate objects or abstract ideas. Many class 5 nouns begin with the letters **j**- or **ji**-

jicho *(eye)* **jengo** *(building)*
jiwe *(rock)*

However, many other class 5 nouns have no recognizable nominal prefix at all.

hitaji *(requirement)* **duka** *(shop)*
shetani *(devil)*

There are a few class 5 nouns that refer to people, but in most grammatical contexts these use class 1 agreements (see CLASS 1 above).

polisi (*policeman*)   **daktari** (*doctor*)

You will learn more about how to use class 5 agreements in Chapters 20 (Subject Prefixes), 34 (Objects), and in the series of chapters on adjectives and pronouns (6-20).

CLASS 6 ngeli ya sita
Nouns in class 6 are the plurals of nouns in class 5, and they usually refer to inanimate objects or abstract ideas. They always begin with the nominal prefix **ma-**

macho (*eyes*)   **majengo** (*buildings*)
maduka (*shops*)   **mawe** (*rocks*)
mashetani (*devils*)
mahitaji (*requirements*)

There are a few class 6 nouns that refer to people, but in most grammatical contexts these use class 2 agreements (see CLASS 2 above).

mapolisi (*policeman*)   **madaktari** (*doctor*)

There are also class 6 nouns that have <u>no</u> class 5 equivalents and can be both singular and plural.

mazingira (*environment*)
mashtaka (*accusations*)
maisha (*life*)
mazishi (*funeral*)

You will learn more about how to use class 6 agreements in Chapters 20 (Subject Prefixes), 34 (Objects), and in the series of chapters on adjectives and pronouns (6-20).

CLASS 7 ngeli ya saba

Nouns in class 7 are singular, and usually refer to inanimate objects, abstract ideas, and languages. They always begin with either **ki-** or **ch-**.

kitabu *(book)*   **chakula** *(food)*
kina *(rhyme)*   **Kiswahili** *(Swahili)*

There are some class 7 nouns refer to people and take class 1 agreements (see CLASS 1 above).

kipofu *(blind person)*
kilema *(a crippled person)*
kifaru *(rhinoceros)*

You will learn more about how to use class 7 agreements in Chapters 20 (Subject Prefixes), 34 (Objects), and in the series of chapters on adjectives and pronouns (6-20).

In some cases, adding the class 7 nominal prefix **ki-** can be used to make a noun of another class diminutive (smaller).

mtoto *(child)* class 1 $\Rightarrow$ **kitoto** *(little child)* class 7

mbuzi *(goat)* class 1 $\Rightarrow$ **kibuzi** *(little goat)* class 7

embe *(mango)* class 5 $\Rightarrow$ **kiembe** *(little mango)* class 7

CLASS 8 ngeli ya nane

Nouns in class 8 are the plurals of nouns in class 7, and they usually refer to inanimate objects or abstract ideas. They always begin with the nominal prefix **vi-** or **vy-**.

vitabu *(books)*   **vyakula** *(foods)*
vina *(rhymes)*

There are some class 8 nouns that refer to people and take class 2 agreements (see CLASS 2 above).

vipofu *(blind people)*
vilema *(crippled people)*
vifaru *(rhinoceroses)*

You will learn more about when they take class 2 agreements in Chapters 20 (Subject Prefixes), 34 (Objects), and in the series of chapters on adjectives and pronouns (6-20).

CLASS 9 *ngeli ya tisa*

Nouns in class 9 are singular, with no recognizable nominal prefix. They usually refer to inanimate objects or abstract ideas.

safari *(journey)*   **kazi** *(work)*

Proper nouns that refer to places are also in class 9.

Tanzania   **Amerika** *(America)*
Zuhura *(the planet Venus)*

Many class 9 nouns are **adopted words,** words that were adopted from other languages into Swahili. These are called **maneno yaliyotoholewa.**

kompyuta *(computer,* from English)
sayari *(planet,* from Arabic)

Many nouns that refer to animals, and some that refer to people, are in class 9, but in most grammatical contexts they are treated as if they were class 1 (see CLASS 1 above).

simba *(lion)*   **mbwa** *(dog)*
baba *(father)*

CLASS 10 ngeli ya kumi

Nouns in class 10 are the plurals of nouns in class 9 and class 11, and they have no recognizable nominal prefix. They usually refer to inanimate objects or abstract ideas.

safari *(journeys)*   **kazi** *(jobs)*

Many class 10 nouns are adopted words.

kompyuta *(computers,* from English)
sayari *(planets,* from Arabic)

Many nouns that refer to animals, and some that refer to people, are in class 10, but in most grammatical contexts they are treated as if they were class 2 (see CLASS 2 above).

simba *(lions)*   **mbwa** *(dogs)*
baba *(fathers)*

CLASS 11 ngeli ya kumi na moja

Nouns in class 11 are singular, with the nominal prefix **u-**. Often they refer to long, thin objects.

ukuta *(wall)*   **ulimi** *(tongue)*
udevu *(whisker)*

CLASS 14 ngeli ya kumi na nne

Nouns in class 14 are abstract ideas. Although class 14 nouns look like class 11 nouns, you can tell the difference because they only exist in the singular; there is no way to make a class 14 noun plural. They begin with the nominal prefix **u-**.

uhuru (*freedom*)   **umoja** (*unity*)
ujamaa (*socialism*)

CLASS 15 ngeli ya kumi na tano

Nouns in class 15 refer to actions. These are **verbal nouns**, also known as **gerunds** or **infinitives**. In Swahili they are known as **vitenzijina**. They begin with the nominal prefix **ku-**, also known as an **infinitive prefix**.

kusoma (*studying*)
kufanya (*doing*)
kupiga (*hitting*)

CLASS 16 ngeli ya kumi na sita

Nouns in class 16, 17 and 18 are called **locatives** because they refer to places. In Swahili they are called **majina ya mahali.** Class 16 nouns refer to places that are specific or close to the speaker; they can be either singular or plural depending on context.

mahali (*place; places*)

Almost any noun from any other noun class can be made into a class 16 noun by adding the locative suffix -**ni**.

nyumba 9/10 (*house*) ⇒ **nyumbani** 16 (*at the house*)

chumba 7 (*room*) ⇒ **chumbani** 16 (*in the room*)

CLASS 17 *ngeli ya kumi na saba*
Nouns in class 17 refer to places that are general or not close to the speaker; they can be either singular or plural depending on context. Almost any noun from any other noun class can be made into a class 17 noun by adding the locative suffix -**ni**.

> **mji** 3 (*city*) ⇒ **mjini** 17 (*in the city*)
> **nchi** 9/10 (*country*) ⇒ **nchini** (*in the country*)

CLASS 18 *ngeli ya kumi na nane*
Nouns in class 18 refer to places that are inside or very close to another object; they can be either singular or plural depending on context. Almost any noun can be made into a class 18 noun by adding the locative suffix -**ni**.

> **mfuko** 3 (*bag*) ⇒ **mfukoni** 18 (*in the bag*)
> **kichwa** 7 (*head*) ⇒ **kichwani** 18 (*on the head*)

As you can see, nouns of class 16, 17 and 18 look the same. The differences between them can be understood by looking for other clues in the sentence.

TAKE NOTE

Like English, Swahili has collective nouns, known as **nomino wingi**. Here are a few examples.

> **familia** (*family or families*; class 9/10)
> **kundi** (*group*; class 5)
> **kamati** (*committee(s)*; class 9/10)

However, in Swahili the number of these words can be treated in one of two ways.

1. A collective noun may be treated as a singular noun of whatever noun class it belongs.

Familia	**inaenda**	**dukani.**
the family	*it is going*	*to the store*

(The family is going to the store.)

Kundi	**linatoa**	**uamuzi**	**wake.**
the group	*it is announcing*	*decision*	*its*

(The group is announcing its decision.)

2. Or a collective noun may be treated as a group of its members.

Familia	**wanaenda**	**pwani.**
family	*they are going*	*to the coast*

(The family is going to the coast.)

In this example the phrase *the people of* is understood but not stated.

(Watu wa)	**familia**	**wanaenda**	**pwani.**
(the people of)	*the family*	*they are going*	*to the coast*

(The family is going to the coast.)

Note that these sentences mean the same thing regardless of how the collective noun is used.

As you learn a new noun, you should always learn its class in both the singular and plural, because its class will affect the spelling and pronunciation of words related to it.

Textbooks and dictionaries usually list words only in the singular. Sometimes they indicate the class of a noun with numbers that indicate both its singular and plural.

mtu 1/2
kifo 7/8
ukuta 11/10

Other times they indicate the class of the noun by providing the plural or the plural nominal prefix.

mtu (watu)	or	**mtu** (wa-)
kifo (vifo)	or	**kifo** (vi-)
ukuta (kuta)		

REVIEW

A. Read out loud the English and Swahili words below. Indicate whether the word is singular (S) or plural (P).

1.	desks	S	P
2.	**msichana** *(girl)*	S	P
3.	**mitihani** *(tests)*	S	P
4.	**mabega** *(shoulders)*	S	P
5.	**paka** *(cats)*	S	P
6.	family	S	P
7.	**ukubwa** *(size)*	S	P
8.	**kitabu** *(book)*	S	P

B. Identify the class of each of these nouns. If there is more than one possible answer, write all of the possible answers.

    a) **kilabu** (*club*) _____

    b) **walimu** (*teachers*) _____

    c) **dirishani** (*in the window*) _____

    d) **ndizi** (*bananas*) _____

    e) **jicho** (*eye*) _____

    f) **uso** (*face*) _____

    g) **miji** (*cities*) _____

    h) **sahani** (*dish*) _____

    i) **maji** (*water*) _____

    j) **mwana** (*son*) _____

    k) **maktabani** (*at the library*) _____

    l) **udogo** (*smallness*) _____

Chapter 4
VERBAL NOUNS

A **verbal noun** is a verb form that is part verb and part noun. It is also known as a **gerund**. Another kind of verb is the **infinitive**, which gives the verb's basic meaning.

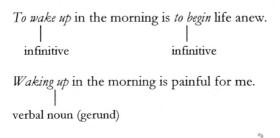

To wake up in the morning is *to begin* life anew.

    infinitive   infinitive

Waking up in the morning is painful for me.

    verbal noun (gerund)

IN ENGLISH
Infinitives
An **infinitive** is a form of the verb without person or number, giving its fundamental meaning. The infinitive is composed of two words, *to* + verb.

    to enjoy   to speak   to fall

When you look up a verb in the dictionary, you find it without the *to*. This form is called the **dictionary form**.

    enjoy   speak   fall

All verbs have a present infinitive and a perfect infinitive. The **present infinitive** is usually *to* + the verb. The **perfect infinitive** is *to have* + the past participle of the main verb.

Present Infinitive	**Perfect Infinitive**
to be	to have been
to borrow	to have borrowed
to say	to have said

The infinitive is generally used with another conjugated verb. You will learn more about conjugated verbs in Chapters 21-44.

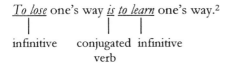

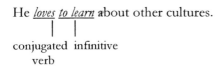

Gerunds

The **gerund**, or verbal noun, is formed from the dictionary form of the verb + *-ing*.

buying
praying
sleeping

It can operate in a sentence in almost any way that a noun can: as a subject, object of a verb, or object of a preposition.

---

[2] A loose translation of the Swahili proverb **Kupotea njia ndiko kujua njia**. The message is that one shouldn't be afraid to try new things or to fail; both are opportunities to learn.

Running is exhilarating.
|
noun from the verb *to run*
subject of the sentence

Juma loves *running*.
|
noun from the verb *to run*
direct object of the verb *to love*

The sport of *running* is competitive.
|
noun from the verb *to run*
object of the preposition *of*

Since the English *–ing* form of the verb can be part of a verb phrase, a verbal adjective (**gerundive** or **present participle;** see Chapter 42), or a verbal noun (gerund), it is important to distinguish among these three uses in order to choose the correct Swahili equivalent.

Mwanaarusi *is visiting* friends.
|
verb phrase
present tense

She is a *loving* mother.
|
verbal adjective (gerundive)
present participle

Seeing is difficult in this fog.
|
verbal noun (gerund)

KWA KISWAHILI

Infinitives and gerunds are the same thing; to avoid confusion, in this book both are referred to as **verbal nouns.** In Swahili they are both called **vitenzijina.** The singular, *infinitive* or *gerund*, is **kitenzijina.** In addition to being verbs, they are also nouns of class 15 (see Chapter 3, Noun Class).

Verbal nouns are composed of one word with the prefix **ku-** + the verb stem.

> **kucheza** *(to play; playing)*
> **kutembea** *(to walk; walking)*
> **kusema** *(to speak; speaking)*

There is only one kind of infinitive, the present infinitive or **kitenzijina cha wakati uliopo.** The main uses of the infinitive/gerund are to complement the meaning of the conjugated verb and to function as a noun.

> **Amina anapenda *kucheza* karata.**
> | |
>   conjugated   infinitive/gerund
>   verb
> (Amina loves *to play* cards; or Amina loves *playing* cards.)

> ***Kuona* kifaru kunavutia.**
> |
> infinitive/gerund
> (*To see* a rhino is interesting; or *Seeing* a rhino is interesting.)

A verbal noun can function in any way that a noun can function.

Kuuliza si ujinga.[3]

|

Subject
(*Asking* is not stupid; or *To ask* is not stupid.)

Sisomi *kuandika* kwake.

|

direct object
(I don't read his *writing*.)

TAKE NOTE

It is important to distinguish between English *–ing* forms. For reference, there is a chart on the next page summarizing the various English *–ing* forms and their Swahili equivalents.

---

[3] A Swahili proverb, which would be literally translated as "Asking is not stupidity."

ENGLISH -ing	SWAHILI EQUIVALENT
Verb phrase	Conjugated verb
auxiliary + present	various tenses
ex: *is reading*	present (**anasoma**)
was reading	past progressive (**alikuwa akisoma**)
will be reading	future progressive (**atakuwa akisoma**)
Adjective	
present participle	Relative or Possessive relative + verbal noun
ex: *loving mother*	(**mama anayependa**)
Thinking about his vacation, he did not work hard in school.	Tenseless participle (Chapter 42) (**Akifikiri kuhusu likizo yake, hakufanya kazi kwa bidii shuleni.**)
Gerund	Verbal Noun
subject of sentence	verbal noun
ex: *Seeing is believing.*	(**Kuona ni kuamini.**)
direct object of sentence	verbal noun
ex: *I don't read his writing.*	(**Sisomi kuandika kwake.**)
other functions	verbal noun
	-**a** or **kwa** + verbal noun
ex: *of* or *by walking*	(**kwa kutembea**)

REVIEW

A. Fill in the blanks using infinitives.

1. **Ninapenda** _____ **mchana.**
   (*I like* _____ *in the afternoon.*)
2. **Je, unataka** _____ **kesho?**
   (*Do you want* _____ *tomorrow?*)
3. He knows how _____ very well.
4. _____ is great fun.
5. **Tumechelewa** _____**dukani.**
   (*We were late* _____ *at the store.*)

B. Underline the *–ing* word in the sentences below. Circle whether the *–ing* word is a gerund (G), an adjective (A), or part of a verb phrase (VP).

1. Wanting to visit her mother, Ashura went to Pemba.

                                G   A   VP

2. The train traveled slowly, never reaching great speeds.

                                G   A   VP

3. Zawadi was always thinking about her studies.

                                G   A   VP

4. By riding her bike, Adija was able to reach school on time.

                                G   A   VP

5. I enjoy swimming in Lake Victoria.

                                G   A   VP

CHAPTER 5
NEGATIVE VERBAL NOUNS

To negate a verb is to make it negative. An **affirmative** verb is one that is not negated.

> I am a student.
> He wanted to be a teacher.
> They will travel on the weekend.

A **negative** verb is one that is negated.

> I am *not* a student.
> He did *not* want to be a teacher.
> They will *not* travel on the weekend.

Like all verbs, a verbal noun (that is, an infinitive or a gerund) can be negated.

> I would prefer *not to swim*.
> *Not asking* would be foolish.

IN ENGLISH

Adding the word *not* before the infinitive or gerund negates a verbal noun.

> to bite $\Rightarrow$ *not* to bite
> biting $\Rightarrow$ *not* biting

KWA KISWAHILI

Inserting the morpheme[4] -to- or -toku- in between the subject marker -*ku*- and the dictionary form of the verb negates a verbal noun.

kupeleka ⟹ **kutopeleka** *or* **kutokupeleka**
sending, to send ⟹ *not sending, not to send*

kufanya ⟹ **kutofanya** *or* **kutokufanya**
doing, to do ⟹ *not doing, not to do*

REVIEW

A. Rewrite the infinitive or gerund in each sentence, putting it in the negative.

1. Do you want to walk?

---

2. Travelling by train is risky.

---

4. While walking, he fell.

---

[4] A *morpheme* is the "smallest linguistic unit which has a meaning or grammatical function." See "Morphology: The Minimal Units of Meaning: Morphemes," *Language Files,* 5th edition, Monica Crabtree & Joyce Powers, compilers (Columbus: Ohio State U. P., 1991): 127.

B. Rewrite the verbal noun in each sentence, putting it in the negative.

1. **Kucheka ni kuzuri.**
   Laughing is good.

   _____

2. **Kamati wanataka kukutana.**
   The committee wants to meet.

   _____

3. **Nilikumbuka kutia chumvi.**
   I remembered to add salt.

   _____

PRONOUNS

Chapter 6
INTRODUCTION TO PRONOUNS

A **pronoun** is a word used in place of one or more nouns. It may stand for a person, place, thing or idea.

For example, instead of repeating the proper noun *Abunawas* in the following sentences, it is preferable to use a pronoun in the second sentence.

> *Abunawas* went to the market. *Abunawas* decided to buy a donkey.
>
> pronoun
|
>
> *Abunawas* went to the market. **He** decided to buy a donkey.

A pronoun can only be used to refer to someone or something that has already been mentioned or is understood. The word that the pronoun replaces or refers to is called the **antecedent** of the pronoun. In the example above, the pronoun *he* refers to the proper noun *Abunawas*. *Abunawas*, therefore, is the antecedent of the pronoun *he*.

IN ENGLISH
There are different types of pronouns. They are described in the following chapters. Listed below are the most important categories and the chapters in which they are discussed in detail.

Personal pronouns (Chapter 7) change in form in the different persons and according to the function they have in the sentence.

- as subject (see Chapter 19); for example:
  I love; *they* walk; *he* bathes; *she* listens.

- as direct object (see Chapter 35); for example:
  Adija buys *it*.
  The boy knows *her*.
  The girl hit *him*.

- as indirect object (see Chapter 36); for example:
  The teacher bought *her* a gift.
  The priest offered *me* advice.
  The farmer sold *us* a cow.

- as object of a preposition (see Chapter 48); for example:
  Go with *them*.
  These are for *you*.
  Sit next to *him*.

Reflexive pronouns (Chapter 8) refer back to the subject of the sentence (see chapter 19).

He helped *himself*.
They relied on *themselves*.
She talks to *herself*.

Interrogative pronouns (Chapter 9) are used in questions at the beginning of the question sentence. They are the first words, unless they are the objects of a preposition (see Chapter 48).

Who is driving the bus?
What are you doing?
Whom will you interview?
To whom are you speaking?

Demonstrative pronouns (Chapter 10) are used to point out people or things.

> *These* are sweet. *Those* are sour.
> *This* is our house. *That* is hers.

Possessive pronouns (Chapter 11) are used to show possession.

> Whose dog is this? It is *hers*.
> *Mine* is the brown dog over there.

Relative pronouns (Chapter 12) are used to introduce relative subordinate clauses (see Chapter 49, Sentences, Phrases and Clauses). For example:

> The car, *which* he bought, is fast.
> The food, *which* they are cooking, smells delicious.

Indefinite pronouns (Chapter 13) indicate certain people or things that are not specified or not clearly seen. For example:

> *Someone* is coming for dinner.
> I gave him *something* for his trouble.

KWA KISWAHILI

These various types of pronouns (with the exception of the reflexive pronouns) also exist in Swahili. They are different from English pronouns, however, because Swahili pronouns always reflect the class of the nouns to which they refer. The next seven chapters will illustrate how the different Swahili pronouns function.

Chapter 7
PERSONAL PRONOUNS

A **personal pronoun** is a word taking the place of a noun that refers to a person or thing.

> *I* am listening to music.
> *We* are leaving tomorrow.
> His parents love *him* very much.
> They watched the movie and enjoyed *it*.

IN ENGLISH
Personal pronouns have distinct forms that show their function in a sentence. Personal pronouns can function as subjects or objects.

Personal Pronouns as Subjects
A different pronoun is used depending on the person referred to (*I* as opposed to *you*) and some pronouns (such as *she* and *they*) indicate whether one person or more than one person is involved in the action of the verb. For example:

> *He* sat, and *they* stood.
> - Who sat? *He* did. *He* is the singular subject of the verb *sat*.
> - Who stood? *They* did. *They* is the plural subject of the verb *stood*.

Here is a list of the pronouns used as subjects:

	SINGULAR	PLURAL
1st person	I	we
2nd person	you	you
3rd person	he/she/it	they

Personal Pronouns as Objects

A different pronoun is used depending on the person referred to (*me* as opposed to *you*) and some pronouns (such as *her* and *them*) indicate whether one person or more than one person is acted upon.

The policeman arrested *her* and *me*.
- The policeman arrested whom? *Her* and *me*. *Her* and *me* are the direct objects of *arrested*.

The doctor spoke to *them* frankly.
- The doctor spoke to whom? *To them*. *Them* is the direct object of *spoke to*.

The students are sitting behind *you* and *him*.
- The students are sitting behind whom? *You* and *him*. *You* and *him* are objects of the preposition *behind*.

Most pronouns that function as objects in a sentence are different from the ones that function as subjects. Compare the subjects and objects in English for the personal pronouns:

SUBJECT	OBJECT
I	me
you	you
he/she/it	him/her/it
we	us
you	you
they	them

Only *you* and *it* have the same form as subjects and objects.

KWA KISWAHILI

Personal pronouns, which are called **viwakilishi nomino vya watu**, are the same whether used as subjects or objects.

Yeye alinipiga. *He hit me.*
Nilimpiga yeye. *I hit him.*

However, Swahili personal pronouns do have different forms depending on the person referred to and whether they are singular or plural.

Here is a list of the personal pronouns used as subjects and objects:

	SINGULAR	PLURAL
1st person	**mimi** *I, me*	**sisi** *we, us*
2nd person	**wewe** *you*	**ninyi** (or **nyinyi**) *you*
3rd person	**yeye** *he, him, she, her*	**wao** *they, them*

The words *it, they,* and *them* are not expressed by personal pronouns in Swahili when they do not refer to people. Instead, demonstrative pronouns are used. Demonstrative pronouns are explained in Chapter 10.

TAKE NOTE

In English there is no difference between *you* in the singular and *you* in the plural. For example, if there were many people present and someone asked aloud, "Are *you* coming with me?" *you* could stand for one person or for many.

In Swahili there is a difference between *you* in the singular and *you* in the plural.

Wewe uende dukani.   *You* (singular)
                              should go to the store.
Ninyi mwende dukani.   *You* (plural) should
                              go to the store.

REVIEW

Write the Swahili personal pronoun you would use to replace
the underlined words in each sentence.

1. <u>We</u> are getting ready for our journey.   _____

2. Would <u>you</u> (pl.) mind helping <u>us</u>?   _____

3. Go to the neighbors and ask <u>them</u> for some bags.

   _____

4. <u>They</u> won't mind loaning us some rope, too.

   _____

5. If they aren't there, ask the man who lives next door. <u>He</u>
   is very nice and I know <u>him</u> well.

   _____

Chapter 8
REFLEXIVE PRONOUNS

A **reflexive pronoun** is a pronoun that is used either as the object of a verb or as the object of a preposition. It is called reflexive because it *reflects* back to the subject.

Tiriza likes to look at *herself* in the mirror.
|
reflexive pronoun

IN ENGLISH

Reflexive pronouns end with *-self* in the singular and *-selves* in the plural.

1ˢᵗ person	myself	ourselves
2ⁿᵈ person	yourself	yourselves
3ʳᵈ person	himself	
	herself	themselves
	itself	

Reflexive pronouns can have a variety of functions: direct and indirect objects, and objects of a preposition.

- He hurt *himself* while exercising.
  He is the subject of *hurt*; *himself* is the direct object.

- They bought *themselves* a new sofa.
  They is the subject of *bought; themselves* is indirect object.

- She is always talking about *herself.*
  She is the subject of *talking; herself* is the object of the preposition *about.*

KWA KISWAHILI

There is no pronoun that serves the same function as the English reflexive pronoun. However, Swahili can express the reflexive meaning by using the object marker **-ji-, shamirisho ya kujirejea,** *the reflexive object marker.*

Nilijilipia ada za shule. *I paid the school fees for <u>myself</u>.*
Ulijisaidia. *You helped <u>yourself</u>.*
Alijiangalia. *He looked at <u>himself</u>.*
Tutajinunulia gari. *We will buy <u>ourselves</u> a car.*
Mnajificha. *You all are hiding <u>yourselves</u>.*
Wanajipikia. *They cook for <u>themselves</u>.*

REVIEW

Translate the following sentences, using the Swahili verbs given. If you are unsure about which subject markers to use, you will need to review Chapter 20, *Subject Prefixes*.

1. He loves himself.
    (**kupenda** *to love*)

    _____

2. Do you understand yourself?
    (**kufahamu** *to understand*)

    _____

3. She trusted herself.
    (**kuamini** *to trust*)

    _____

4. They rely on themselves.
    (**kutegemea** *to rely*)

    _____

5. Can you all read to yourselves?
    (**kusomea** *to read to*)

    _____

Chapter 9
INTERROGATIVE PRONOUNS

An **interrogative pronoun** is a pronoun that introduces a question. *Interrogative* comes from the verb *to interrogate*, which means *to question*. Here are some examples of interrogative pronouns used in questions.

> *Who* is going to the cinema?
> |
> replaces a person

> *What* did you eat yesterday?
> |
> replaces a thing

In both Swahili and English, a different interrogative pronoun is used depending on whether it refers to a person or a thing. The form of the interrogative pronoun also sometimes changes according to the function the pronoun performs in the sentence. For example, the interrogative pronoun could function as the subject, direct object, indirect object or object of the preposition.

IN ENGLISH
Different interrogative pronouns are used for asking about people or things.

> *Who* wants dessert?
> *What* is your name?

Asking about People
The interrogative pronoun to ask about people has three different forms depending on its function in the sentence.

1. *Who* is used for the subject of the sentence.

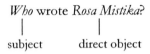

Who wrote *Rosa Mistika?*
| |
subject   direct object

2. *Whom* is the form used for the direct or indirect object of the sentence, or with the object of a preposition.

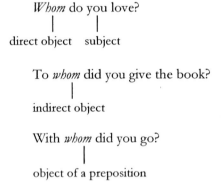

Whom do you love?
| |
direct object   subject

To *whom* did you give the book?
|
indirect object

With *whom* did you go?
|
object of a preposition

3. *Whose* is the possessive form and is used to ask about possession or ownership.

Look at that beautiful garden. *Whose* is it?

Whose can refer to one or more persons.

Whose are these books?
- They are the student's. (singular answer)
- They are the students'. (plural answer)

Asking about Things

What is used to ask about things. It does not change forms.

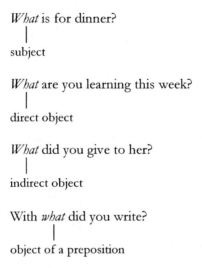

What is for dinner?

subject

What are you learning this week?

direct object

What did you give to her?

indirect object

With *what* did you write?

object of a preposition

What is considered singular when followed by a singular verb.
The answer can be singular or plural.

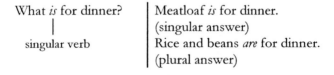

What *is* for dinner?	Meatloaf *is* for dinner.
singular verb	(singular answer)
	Rice and beans *are* for dinner.
	(plural answer)

KWA KISWAHILI

As in English, different interrogative pronouns are used for
asking about people or things.

<u>Nani</u> anasikiliza redio?
<u>Who</u> is listening to the radio?
<u>Nini</u> kilitokea? (Kitu gani kilitokea?)
<u>What</u> happened? (What thing happened?)

Asking about People

The interrogative pronoun to ask about people has two different forms depending on whether it is singular or plural. Both forms can be used as subject, direct object, indirect object or object of a preposition. Generally they precede the verb if functioning as a subject and follow the verb if functioning as an object.

Nani is used when a singular answer is expected.

1. It can be used as a subject of a question. For example:

> **Nani atakuja kesho?** *Who will come tomorrow?*
> **Juma atakuja kesho.** *Juma will come tomorrow.*
> (singular answer)

2. It can be used as a direct object. For example:

> **Ulimwona nani?** *Whom did you see?*
> **Nilimwona Salma.** *I saw Salma.* (singular answer)

3. It can be used as an indirect object. For example:

> **Alimpa nani barua?** *To whom did she give a letter?*
> **Alinipa mimi.** *She gave a letter to me.* (singular answer)

4. It can be used as an object of a preposition. For example:

> **Utasafiri na nani?** With *whom* will you travel?
> **Nitasafiri na Sudi.** *I will travel with Sudi.*
> (singular answer)

Note that **nani** always take class 1 noun agreements, i.e. the **a-** subject marker and the **-mw-** object marker.

Akina nani is used when a plural answer is expected.

1. It can be used as a subject of a question. For example:

> **Akina nani watakuja kesho?**
> *Who will come tomorrow?*
> **Ali na babake watakuja kesho.**
> *Ali and his father will come tomorrow.* (plural answer)

2. It can be used as a direct object. For example:

> **Tutawatembelea akina nani?**
> *Whom will we visit?*
> **Tutawatembelea wanafunzi.**
> *We will visit the students.* (plural answer)

3. It can be used as an indirect object. For example:

> **Waliwapa akina nani zawadi?**
> *To whom did they give gifts?*
> **Waliwapa watoto zawadi.**
> *They gave gifts to the children.* (plural answer)

4. It can be used as an object of a preposition. For example:

> **Mtawapikia akina nani?**
> *For whom will you all cook?*
> **Tutawapikia rafiki zetu.**
> *We will cook for our friends.* (plural answer)

Note that **akina nani** always takes class 2 noun agreements, i.e. the **wa-** subject marker and the **-wa-** object marker.

Both **nani** and **akina nani** can be used as possessive forms by combining them with the preposition **-a** (*of*).

Kitabu hiki ni <u>cha nani</u>?
Whose book is this?
Nyumba hizi ni <u>za akina nani</u>?
Whose houses are these?

Note that the preposition -**a** must always agree with the class of the noun to which it refers. It takes the same set of class prefixes as possessive adjectives (see Chapter 16).

Asking about Things
Nini is used to ask about things. It is the same for the singular or the plural, and can function as the subject, direct object, indirect object or object of a preposition. Generally it precedes the verb if functioning as a subject and follows the verb if functioning as an object.

(Kitu gani kinakusumbua?)
(What thing is bothering you?)

<u>Nini</u> kinakusumbua? *<u>What</u> is bothering you?*
|
subject

Unataka <u>nini</u>? *<u>What</u> do you want?*
|
direct object

Alikupa <u>nini</u>? *<u>What</u> did she give to you?*

indirect object

Mtaenda na <u>nini</u>? *With what will you all go?*

object of a preposition

Do not confuse the **interrogative adjective**s with the **interrogative pronouns**. Interrogative adjectives (Chapter 17) always accompany a noun, while pronouns stand alone.

two types of *whose*

Whose bag is this?
- *Whose* is an interrogative adjective modifying the noun *bag.*
- **Mfuko huu ni wa nani?**

I found this bag; *whose* is it?
- *Whose* is an interrogative pronoun modifying the noun *bag.*
- **Nilikuta mfuko huu; ni wa nani?**

In Swahili the interrogative adjective that means *whose* (-**a nani**) takes the same form as the interrogative pronoun *whose* (-**a nani**). It is an adjective if it follows a noun, but a pronoun if it stands alone.

two types of *what*

What book are you reading?
- *What* is an interrogative adjective modifying the noun *book*.
- **Unasoma kitabu <u>gani</u>?**

What are you reading?
- *What* is an interrogative pronoun standing in for the word *book*.
- **Unasoma <u>nini</u>?**

If *what* precedes a noun, it is an interrogative adjective. If it stands alone, it is an interrogative pronoun.

In Swahili, **gani** follows the noun it modifies, while **nini** stands alone. Thus **gani** is an interrogative adjective, while **nini** is an interrogative pronoun.

REVIEW

Underline the interrogative adjectives and interrogative pronouns in the sentences below. Circle whether each word that you underline is an interrogative adjective (A) or an interrogative pronoun (P) and — if applicable — a subject (S) or object (O). You should be able to do this even if you don't understand all the words in the Swahili sentences.

1. *What do you want to do in Zanzibar?*

   A   P   S   O

2. *What towns will you visit?*

   A   P   S   O

3. *With whom will you travel?*

   A   P   S   O

4. *Whose suitcase is this?*

   A   P   S   O

5. *Whom will you stay with?*

   A   P   S   O

6. **Nani anaenda nawe?**

   A   P   S   O

7. **Mtanunua zawadi gani?**

   A   P   S   O

8. **Wewe ni mtalii wa aina gani?**

   A   P   S   O

9. **Akina nani wanakulipia safari yako?**

A   P   S   O

10. **Utafanya nini baada ya safari yako?**

A   P   S   O

Chapter 10
DEMONSTRATIVE PRONOUNS

A **demonstrative pronoun** replaces a noun that has been mentioned previously or is understood. It is called demonstrative because it points out a person or thing. The word *demonstrative* comes from the verb *to demonstrate*, which means *to show*.

IN ENGLISH

The demonstrative pronouns are *this (one)* and *that (one)* in the singular and *these* and *those* in the plural.

The distinction between *this* and *that* can be used to contrast one object or person from another, or to refer to things that are not the same distance away. The speaker uses *this* or *these* for the closer objects and *that* or *those* for the ones farther away.

> We have two sons. *This* (one) is Hud; *that* (one) is Assim.
> *These* are our fields. *Those* are the neighbor's.

KWA KISWAHILI

Demonstrative pronouns are called **vionyeshi** in Swahili. The singular, *demonstrative pronoun*, is called **kionyeshi.** Here are some examples of demonstrative pronouns used in sentences:

Nina zawadi mbili kwa familia yako. Hii ni kwa wazee na ile ni kwa watoto.
I have two gifts for your family. This is for the elders and that is for the children.

Hawa ni watoto wangu. Wale ni wa dada yangu.
These are my children. Those are my sister's.

There are three types of Swahili demonstrative pronouns. The one used depends on the distance between the speaker or hearer and the object or person pointed out, as well as on whether this is the first time the object or person is being mentioned or a reference to someone or something that has already been mentioned. All demonstrative adjectives must agree with the noun they refer to, using a system of class agreements.

Demonstrative pronouns use the same three sets of forms as demonstrative adjectives, which are explained in Chapter 18. For this reason, they are sometimes referred to simply as **demonstratives**. In Swahili, both are called **vionyeshi.** The difference is that demonstrative adjectives always follow the noun they modify, while pronouns stand in for the nouns they refer to.

1. The first type of demonstrative adjective is equivalent to the English demonstratives *this* or *these*. It is used exactly as *this* and *these* are used in English.

CLASS	DEMONSTRATIVE PRONOUN	ENGLISH TRANSLATION
1	**huyu**	*this (person)*
2	**hawa**	*these (people)*
3	**huu**	*this (thing)*
4	**hii**	*these (things)*
5	**hili**	*this (thing)*
6	**haya**	*these (things)*
7	**hiki**	*this (thing)*
8	**hivi**	*these (things)*
9	**hii**	*this (thing)*
10	**hizi**	*these (things)*
11	**huu**	*this (thing)*
14	**huu**	*this (thing)*
15	**huku**	*this (action)*
16	**hapa**	*this (specific place)*
17	**huku**	*this (general place)*
18	**humu**	*this (inside place)*

While you should try to memorize the demonstrative for each class, you will learn them much faster if you understand how they are formed by studying patterns in the chart above.

All of the demonstratives that mean *this* or *these* begin with the letter *h* and end with the same syllable used as a subject prefix in verbs (see Chapter 20, Subject Prefixes). The one exception is in class 1, where the syllable *yu-* is used rather than the subject prefix *a-*. The sound in between the *h* and the subject prefix is always the same as the final vowel.

Here are a few examples of how this demonstrative is formed in different classes. Try to see the pattern for the other classes.

class 1 h- + -u- + -yu = **huyu**
class 5 h- + -i- + -li = **hili**
class 14 h- + -u- + -u = **huu**
class 16 h- + -a- + -pa = **hapa**

2. The second type of demonstrative is equivalent to the
    English demonstratives *that* or *those,* and is used to refer
    to people or things that are distant from the speaker and
    hearer.

CLASS	DEMONSTRATIVE PRONOUN	ENGLISH TRANSLATION
1	**yule**	*that (person) over there*
2	**wale**	*those (people) over there*
3	**ule**	*that (thing) over there*
4	**ile**	*those (things) over there*
5	**lile**	*that (thing) over there*
6	**yale**	*those (things) over there*
7	**kile**	*that (thing) over there*
8	**vile**	*those (things) over there*
9	**ile**	*that (thing) over there*
10	**zile**	*those (things) over there*
11	**ule**	*that (thing) over there*
14	**ule**	*that (thing) over there*
15	**kule**	*that (thing) over there*
16	**pale**	*that (specific place) over there*
17	**kule**	*that (general place) over there*
18	**mle**	*that (inside place) over there*

While you should try to memorize the demonstrative for each class, you will learn them much faster if you understand how they are formed by studying patterns in the chart above.

All of the demonstratives that mean *these* or *those objects or people mentioned earlier* begin with the same subject prefixes used with verbs (see Chapter 20, Subject Prefixes) and end with the syllable -**le.** The one exception is in class 1, where the syllable **yu-** is used rather than the subject prefix **a-**.

Here are a few examples of how this demonstrative is formed in different classes. Try to see the pattern for the other classes.

class 2	*wa-* + *-le* =	**wale**
class 4	*i-* + *-le* =	**ile**
class 7	*ki-* + *-le* =	**kile**
class 18	*m-* + *-le* =	**mle**

3. The third type of demonstrative is also equivalent to the English demonstrative *that* or *those,* but it is used to refer to a person or thing that has been previously mentioned. This type of demonstrative is also used to refer to people or things closer to the hearer and far from the speaker.

CLASS	DEMONSTRATIVE PRONOUN	ENGLISH TRANSLATION
1	huyo	that (person) mentioned earlier
2	hao	those (people) mentioned earlier
3	huo	that (thing) mentioned earlier
4	hiyo	those (things) mentioned earlier
5	hilo	that (thing) mentioned earlier
6	hayo	those (things) mentioned earlier
7	hicho	that (thing) mentioned earlier
8	hivyo	those (things) mentioned earlier
9	hiyo	that (thing) mentioned earlier
10	hizo	those (things) mentioned earlier
11	huo	that (thing) mentioned earlier
14	huo	that (thing) mentioned earlier
15	huko	that (action) mentioned earlier
16	hapo	that (specific place) mentioned earlier
17	huko	that (general place) mentioned earlier
18	humo	that (inside place) mentioned earlier

While you should try to memorize the demonstrative for each class, you will learn them much faster if you understand how they are formed by studying patterns in the chart above.

All of the demonstratives that mean *these* or *those objects or people mentioned earlier* follow the pattern of the demonstratives that mean *this* or *these,* except that the final vowel changes to -o.

Here are a few examples of how this demonstrative is formed in different classes. Try to see the pattern for the other classes.

class 1	**huyu**	⇒ **huyo**
class 3	**huu**	⇒ **huo**
class 10	**hizi**	⇒ **hizo**
class 17	**huku**	⇒ **huko**

Note that in classes 4, 7, 8, and 9 the vowel change (from -**i** to -**o**) results in a sound change in the preceding consonant(s).

class 4 & 9	**hii**	⇒ **hiyo**
class 7	**hiki**	⇒ **hicho**
class 8	**hivi**	⇒ **hivyo**

REVIEW

Underline the demonstratives in the sentences below. Circle whether each is a demonstrative adjective (A) or pronoun (P).

1. *This is not what I expected.*　　　　　A　P

2. *Those cookies are delicious.*　　　　　A　P

3. *What do you think of these?*　　　　　A　P

4. *I haven't tried those yet.*　　　　　A　P

5. *When did you find time to cook all this food?*　　　　　A　P

6. **Pati hii ni nzuri sana; watu
   wengi wapo.**   A   P

7. **Huyo ni nani?**   A   P

8. **Yule ni kakangu.**   A   P

9. **Alileta hiki?**   A   P

10. **Sivyo; alileta chakula hicho.**   A   P

Chapter 11
POSSESSIVE PRONOUNS

A **possessive pronoun** is a word that replaces a noun and that also shows who possesses that noun.

> This house is *ours.*

In this example, *ours* is a pronoun that replaces the noun *house* and that shows who possesses that noun.

IN ENGLISH
Possessive pronouns only agree with the person who possesses, not to the object possessed.

> Is this your house? No, it is not *ours.*
> Are these your eggs? No, they are not *ours.*

In these two examples, the same possessive pronoun *ours* is used, although the object possessed is singular (*house*) in the first sentence and plural (*eggs*) in the second.

Here is a list of the English possessive pronouns:

	SINGULAR	PLURAL
1st person	mine	ours
2nd person	yours	yours
3rd person	his/hers/its	theirs

KWA KISWAHILI

Possessive pronouns are called **vimilikishi**. The singular, *possessive pronoun*, is **kimilikishi**. Here are some examples of possessive pronouns used in sentences:

Kitabu hiki ni <u>changu</u>. *This book is <u>mine</u>.*

Skati lake ni buluu; <u>langu</u> ni nyekundu.
Her skirt is blue; <u>mine</u> is red.

While the English possessive pronouns differ from possessive adjectives, Swahili possessive pronouns and adjectives take exactly the same forms. Both, therefore, are called **vimilikishi**. Here are the forms of the possessive pronouns (and adjectives):

CLASS	POSSESSIVE PREFIX	SWAHILI EXAMPLE	ENGLISH TRANSLATION
1	w-	wangu	*mine*
2	w-	wangu	*mine*
3	w-	wangu	*mine*
4	y-	yangu	*mine*
5	l-	langu	*mine*
6	y-	yangu	*mine*
7	ch-	changu	*mine*
8	vy-	vyangu	*mine*
9	y-	yangu	*mine*
10	z-	zangu	*mine*
11	w-	wangu	*mine*
14	w-	wangu	*mine*
15	kw-	kwangu	*mine*
16	p-	pangu	*at my place*
17	kw-	kwangu	*at my place*
18	mw-	mwangu	*inside my place*

The other possessive adjective roots use the same possessive prefixes listed here to form possessive adjectives.

The same prefixes are used to express the possessive preposition *of*, with the root *-a* followed by the possessor.

CLASS	SWAHILI EXAMPLE	ENGLISH TRANSLATION
1	**wa Juma**	*Juma's*
2	**wa Juma**	*Juma's*
3	**wa Zakia**	*Zakia's*
4	**ya Zakia**	*Zakia's*
5	**la mwalimu**	*the teacher's*
6	**ya walimu**	*the teachers'*
7	**cha daktari**	*the doctor's*
8	**vya daktari**	*the doctor's*
9	**ya rais**	*the president's*
10	**za rais**	*the president's*
11	**wa mbwa**	*the dog's*
14	**wa nchi**	*the country's*
15	**kwa Musa**	*Musa's*
16	**pa Sudi**	*at Sudi's*
17	**kwa Sudi**	*at Sudi's*
18	**mwa Sudi**	*in Sudi's*

The difference between possessive pronouns and adjectives is that possessive adjectives always follow the nouns they modify, while possessive pronouns stand in for the nouns they refer to; both must agree in class with the nouns to which they refer. For example:

Kamusi yangu imepotea. *My dictionary is lost.*

        |

    possessive adjective modifying **kamusi**

Je, una kamusi?   *Do you have a dictionary?*
Yangu imepotea.   *Mine is lost.*

  |

    possessive pronoun, standing in for **kamusi**

REVIEW

Underline the possessives in the sentences below.   Circle
whether the possessive is a pronoun (P) or an adjective (A).

1.	*How old are your children?*	A	P
2.	*Five and seven. And yours?*	A	P
3.	*My son is ten and my daughter is three.*	A	P
4.	*Mine are both girls.*	A	P
5.	*What are their favorite activities?*	A	P
6.	**Wanapenda kucheza na mpira wao.**	A	P
7.	**Ulinunua wao wapi?**	A	P
8.	**Duka lile lile ambapo ulinunua wenu.**	A	P
9.	**Duka lake Ali?**	A	P
10.	**Sivyo; lake Musa.**	A	P

Chapter 12
RELATIVE PRONOUNS/CONSTRUCTIONS

A **relative pronoun** is a word that can serve two purposes:

1. As a pronoun, it stands for a noun or another pronoun previously mentioned, the **antecedent**.

    The food (*that*) you want is not available.

2. It introduces a **subordinate clause**, a group of words having a subject and verb separate from the subject and verb of the main clause. A main clause can stand alone as a complete sentence, but a subordinate clause cannot. See Chapter 49 (Sentences, Phrases and Clauses).

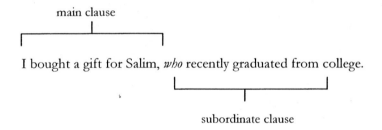

The subordinate clause in this example is also called a relative clause because it starts with a relative pronoun (*who*). The relative clause gives us additional information about the antecedent (*Salim*).

IN ENGLISH

The most frequently used relative pronouns are *who, that, which* and *what*. Different relative pronouns are used according to whether they refer to a person or to a thing.

Referring to a Person

The relative pronoun *who* is used when the antecedent is a person.

Who can be used with both restrictive and non-restrictive clauses. A **restrictive clause** is one that is essential to the meaning of the sentence. A **non-restrictive clause** is one that functions as a parenthetical comment and is usually set off by commas; it is not essential to the meaning of the sentence.

Did you see the man who was just here?

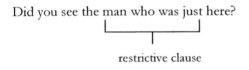

restrictive clause

Adija, (*who* is) a friend of ours, is coming to visit.

non-restrictive clause

Who is the only relative pronoun that changes its form depending on its function in the relative clause. *Who* has five forms used in three different functions: *who, whoever, whom, whomever,* and *whose.*

- *Who* and *whoever* are the forms used as the subjects of the relative clause.

  She married a man *who* truly loved her.
  A. *Who* is the subject of *loved*.

  Student loans are available to *whoever* needs them.
  B. *Whoever* is the subject of *needs*.

- *Whom* and *whomever* are the forms used as the objects of the relative clause. In these examples it is between parentheses because it is often omitted.

  This is the friend about *whom* I was telling you.
  A. *Whom* is the object of the preposition *about*.

  We can invite *whomever* you would like.
  B. *Whomever* is the direct object of the verb *invite*.

- *Whose* is the possessive form.

  Abunawas is a character *whose* stories are well-known.

Referring to Things

The relative pronouns *which* or *that* are used when the antecedent is a thing. They do not change forms.

That is used only when the relative clause is a restrictive clause. Here it is in parentheses because it is often omitted.

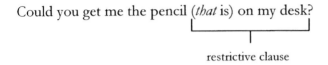

restrictive clause

Which is used only when the relative clause is a non-restrictive clause.

Those shoes, *which* Zawadi bought last week, are too small for her.

non-restrictive clause

KWA KISWAHILI

There are three kinds of relative constructions, which are called **virejeshi**. All relative constructions must agree in class with their antecedents. Each of the three relative constructions can be used to translate all of the English relative pronouns.

Here are the forms that mark agreement. In some cases they serve as suffixes; in other cases they serve as infixes.

CLASS	RELATIVE SUFFIX	RELATIVE INFIX
51	-ye	-ye-
2	-o	-o-
3	-o	-o-
4	-yo	-yo-
5	-lo	-lo-
6	-yo	-yo-
7	-cho	-cho-
8	-vyo	-vyo-
9	-yo	-yo-
10	-zo	-zo-
11	-o	-o-
14	-o	-o-
15	-ko	-ko-
16	-po	-po-
17	-ko	-ko-
18	-mo	-mo-

The *amba-* construction

The only relative construction that is actually a pronoun is *amba-*, which takes a relative suffix. Note that *amba-* can be used with the same meaning as the English forms *who, whom, whose, that* and *which*.

- **Nina rafiki <u>ambaye</u> anakaa huko Uganda.**
  (class 1)
  I have a friend <u>who</u> lives in Uganda.
- **Nina rafiki <u>ambaye</u> nitamtembelea mwezi ujao.**
  (class 1)
  I have a friend <u>whom</u> I will visit next month.
- **Nina rafiki <u>ambaye</u> jina lake ni Sudi.**
  (class 1)
  I have a friend <u>whose</u> name is Sudi.
- **Niliona mti <u>ambao</u> ulianguka.** (class 3)
  I saw a tree <u>that</u> had fallen down.

- **Mti <u>ambao</u> ulianguka ni mkubwa.** (class 3)
  The tree, <u>which</u> fell down, is big.

Infixed relative

A second form of the Swahili relative is the **infixed relative** or **kirejeshi-kati**, in which the relative form functions as a verbal infix. The infix occurs in a verb after the tense marker and before the verb root.

nina + ye + enda = **ninayeenda** *I who go*

The infixed relative cannot be used with the perfect tense (Chapter 26) or the -**a**- tense (Chapter 22). The future tense takes a modified form when used with the infixed relative; the infix -**ka**- occurs after the future tense marker and before the relative infix.

nitaenda *I will go*   **nitakayeenda**
                                  nita + ka + ye + enda
                                  I who will go

Note that the infixed relative can be used with the same meaning as the English forms *who, whom, that* and *which*.

- **Nina rafiki <u>anayekaa</u> huko Uganda.** (class 1)
  I have a friend <u>who lives</u> in Uganda.
- **Nina rafiki <u>nitakayemtembelea</u> mwezi ujao.** (class 1)
  I have a friend <u>whom I will visit</u> next month.
- **Niliona mti <u>ulioanguka</u>.** (class 3)
  I saw a tree <u>that had fallen down</u>.
- **Mti <u>ulioanguka</u> ni mkubwa.** (class 3)
  The tree, <u>which fell down</u>, is big.

Compare these four sentences to those given above that contain the *amba-* relative. Note that the sentences express the same meanings.

Tenseless relative

A third form of the Swahili relative is the **tenseless relative**, or **kirejeshi bila tensi**, in which the relative form functions as a verbal suffix. The verb contains no tense marker and the relative form occurs after the verb root.

li + jengwa + lo = **lijengwalo** *which is built* (class 5)

Because this kind of relative is tenseless, it expresses an activity or state that happens regularly or continuously. Note that the tenseless relative can be used with the same meaning as the English forms *who, whom, that.*

- **Nina rafiki <u>akaaye</u> huko Uganda.** (class 1)
  I have a friend <u>who lives</u> in Uganda.
- **Nina rafiki <u>nimtembeleaye</u> mara kwa mara.** (class 1)
  I have a friend <u>whom I visit</u> often.
- **Ana magari <u>yaharibikayo</u> kila wiki.** (class 6)
  He has cars <u>that break</u> every week.

TAKE NOTE

The three forms of the Swahili relative can, for the most part, be used interchangeably. However, you should keep a few differences in mind that affect how often each form is used:

1. It takes longer to say **amba** + a verb than it does to say a verb with the relative form infixed or suffixed.
2. If you want to use a past or future tense, the tenseless relative cannot be used.

3. If you want to use the perfect tense or simple present, you must use the **amba-** relative.

When the relative form is used as a direct object, and its antecedent is a person, an object marker must also be used. See Chapter 34, Objects, to review object markers.

Use of the Relative Construction
The relative pronoun enables you to combine two short simple sentences into one complex sentence.

The relative as subject

> A. **Shakila ni msichana hodari.**
>   *Shakila is an intelligent girl.*
> B. **Atashinda.**
>   *She will be successful.*

You can combine sentence A with sentence B by replacing the subject *she* with the relative construction in Swahili or with the pronoun *who* in English.

> **Shakila ni msichana hodari <u>ambaye</u> atashinda.**
> *Shakila is an intelligent girl <u>who</u> will be successful.*

Ambaye atashinda or *who will be successful* is the relative clause. It does not express a complete thought, and it is introduced by a relative pronoun.

Ambaye or *who* stands for the noun **msichana** or *girl.* **Msichana** or *girl* is the antecedent of **ambaye** or who. Notice that it stands immediately before the relative pronoun, which introduces the clause and gives additional information about the antecedent.

Ambaye or *who* serves as the subject of the verb **atashinda** in Swahili or *will be* in the relative clause.

The relative as object

  A. **Shakila ni msichana hodari.**
     Shakila is an intelligent girl.
  B. **Mwalimu anampenda Shakila.**
     The teacher likes Shakila.

You can combine sentence A and sentence B by replacing the object **Shakila** with the relative pronoun *whom*.

Shakila, <u>ambaye</u> mwalimu anampenda, ni msichana hodari.
Shakila, <u>whom</u> the teacher likes, is an intelligent girl.

Ambaye mwalimu anampenda or *whom the teacher likes* is the relative clause. **Ambaye** or *whom* stands for the proper noun **Shakila**. **Shakila** is the antecedent. Notice again that the antecedent comes immediately before the relative pronoun.

Ambaye or *whom* serves as the direct object of the relative clause. (**Mwalimu** or *the teacher* is the subject.)

The relative as object of a preposition

A. Shakila ni msichana mwenye hodari.
  Shakila is an intelligent girl.
B. Nilienda shuleni naye.
  I went to school with her.

You can combine sentence A and sentence B by replacing the personal pronoun *her* with the relative pronoun *whom*.

Shakila ni msichana hodari niliyeenda shuleni naye.
Shakila is an intelligent girl with whom I went to school.

Niliyeenda shuleni naye or *with whom I went to school* is the relative clause.

The infix *-ye-* or *whom* stands for the noun **msichana** or *girl*. **Msichana** or *girl* is the antecedent. Notice again that the antecedent comes immediately before the relative pronoun.

TAKE NOTE

In English, relative pronouns are often omitted. It is important that you reinstate them because they must be expressed in Swahili. Restructuring English sentences that contain a dangling preposition will help you to identify relative clauses.

COLLOQUIAL ENGLISH	GRAMMATICALLY CORRECT ENGLISH
Salma is the woman I told you about.	Salma is the woman about whom I told you.

GRAMMATICALLY CORRECT SWAHILI

Salma ni mwanamke ambaye nilikuzungumzia.
(literally: Salma is the woman whom I was discussing about with you.)
OR
Salma ni mwanamke ambaye nilikuambia habari zake.
(literally: Salma is the woman whom I was telling you about (her news).)

REVIEW

Restructure the sentences below to avoid dangling prepositions.

1. Dar es Salaam is the city ^(to which) we are going to.

   Dar ni mji tunayoenda

2. Those girls are the ones ^(to which) I was talking to.

   Wasichana wale ndio niliwazungumza

3. This is the road ^(on which) we should be driving on.

   Hiyo ndiyo barabara tuendeshe

4. This umbrella is not the one ^(w/ which) I came with.

   Umbrella hii siyo

Chapter 13
INDEFINITE PRONOUNS

An **indefinite pronoun** indicates people or things but does not refer to specific people or things.

> *Someone* called while you were gone.
> Accidents can happen to *anyone*.
> *No one* is here.
> *Nothing* is happening this weekend.

IN ENGLISH
The indefinite pronouns include *all, any, both, each, either, neither, everyone, everybody, everything, none, one, several, some, someone, somebody, something, few, many, several, most, another, others, anyone, anybody,* and *anything*.

Note that many of these words can be either pronouns or adjectives, depending on their use in the sentence.

> *Both* of you are invited. (pronoun)
> *Both* students are invited. (adjective)

When the indefinite pronoun is the subject of a sentence, it usually takes a singular verb and any other pronoun referring to it agrees with it in number and gender. When gender may be either masculine or feminine, both pronouns may be used.

> *Each* of us must pay for *him* or *herself*.
> Have *any* of the mothers brought *her* children?

Some indefinite pronouns, such as *everyone, everybody, everything, all,* and *some* can take either a singular or plural verb or pronoun.

Everyone wants to visit Zanzibar during his or her vacation. (singular)
Everyone will come, but they may not stay. (plural)

When the indefinite pronoun is plural in meaning, such as *both, few, many, most* and *several,* it takes a plural verb and is referred to by a plural pronoun.

Most of the workers received *their* paychecks.

KWA KISWAHILI

The indefinite pronouns include -**ote** *(all),* -**o** -**ote** *(any),* -**ote** -**pili** *(both),* -**ingi** *(many),* -**ingine** *(another, others),* **baadhi ya** *(some of),* -**mojawapo** *(one)* and **kadhaa** *(several),* where the hyphen (-) indicates that the pronoun agrees in class with the noun to which it refers.

With the exception of **baadhi ya**, all of these words can be either pronouns or adjectives, depending on their use in the sentence.

Unataka cho chote? *Do you want anything?* (pronoun)
Unataka kitu cho chote? *Do you want anything?* (adjective)

You may note that the number of Swahili indefinite pronouns is much smaller than the number of English pronouns. Many of the concepts that are expressed by indefinite pronouns in English are expressed with other parts of speech in Swahili. Take note of the following (near) equivalents.

each = kila	**Kila** **mtu** alipenda matokeo.[5] *Each (person) liked the results.* (adjective)
everyone = **kila mtu** *(each person)*	**Kila mtu** anahudhuria shule. *Everyone attends school.* (noun phrase)
everything = **kila kitu** *(each thing)*	**Kila kitu** kipo.[6] *Everything is here.* (noun phrase)
or **vitu vyote** *(all things)*	**Vitu vyote** vipo. *Everything is here.* (noun phrase)
or **kila jambo** *(each thing)*	**Kila jambo** lilitokea kwa haraka. Everything happened quickly. (noun phrase)
or **mambo yote** *(all things)*	**Mambo yote** yalitokea kwa haraka. *Everything happened quickly.* (noun phrase)
either = **-o -ote** *(any)*	**Jibu** **lo lote** ni sawa. Either answer is correct. (adjective)
or **-mojawapo** *(one of)*	**Chagua kikapu** **kimojawapo**. *Choose either basket.* (adjective)
neither = **hapana -moja** **+ relative**	**Hapana mmoja** aliyeishi hapa. Neither (person) lived here. (clause)
someone = **mtu fulani** *(a certain person)*	**Mtu fulani** alikuja kukuona. Someone came to see you. (noun phrase)

---

[5] **Kila** is used only with singular nouns, and is one of the few Swahili adjectives that precedes the nouns it modifies.

[6] **Kitu** (plural: **vitu**) is used for a thing that is an object; while **jambo** (plural: **mambo**) is used for a thing that is abstract.

something = **kitu fulani** *(a certain thing)*	**Alinipa <u>kitu fulani.</u>** *She gave me something.* (noun phrase)
or **kitu** *(thing)*	**Alinipa kitu.** *She gave me something.* (noun phrase)
or **jambo fulani** *(a certain thing)*	**<u>Jambo fulani</u> lilitokea hapa.** *Something happened here.* (noun phrase)
or **jambo** *(a thing)*	**<u>Jambo</u> lilitokea hapa.** *Something happened here.* (noun phrase)
most = **karibu kila** *(nearly each)*	**<u>Karibu kila</u> mtu alikuja.** *Most people came.* (adjective phrase)
or **karibu -ote** *(nearly all)*	**<u>Karibu</u> watu <u>wote</u> walikuja.** *Most people came.* (adjective phrase)

REVIEW

Underline the pronouns in each of the sentences below. Indicate whether it is indefinite.

1.   Is anyone coming to class today?

Indefinite?   Yes   No

2.   No, everyone has left for vacation.

Indefinite?   Yes   No

3.   What about Juma? Has anyone seen him?

Indefinite?   Yes   No

4.   I saw him, but he told me he wasn't feeling well.

Indefinite?   Yes   No

5.   Who else is coming besides you?

Indefinite?   Yes   No

ADJECTIVES

Chapter 14
INTRODUCTION TO ADJECTIVES

An **adjective,** called **kivumishi** in Swahili, is a word that describes or modifies a noun or pronoun. Be careful not to confuse an adjective with a pronoun. A pronoun replaces a noun, but an adjective must always have a noun or pronoun to describe.

Listed below are the various types of adjectives and the chapters where they are discussed.

In both English and Swahili, adjectives are classified according to the way they describe a noun or pronoun.

A **descriptive adjective** indicates the quality of someone or something. See Chapter 15, *Descriptive Adjectives.*

> Tatu is playing with a *red* ball.
> The room is *small.*

A **possessive adjective** shows who possesses someone or something. See Chapter 16, *Possessive Adjectives.*

> Sijali is talking to *his* father.
> *Your* sister is beatiful.

An **interrogative adjective** asks a question about someone or something. See Chapter 17, *Interrogative Adjectives.*

> *Which* boy wrote her a letter?
> *What* time do you want to leave?

A **demonstrative adjective** points out someone or something. See Chapter 18, *Demonstrative Adjectives.*

> I want to buy *this* apple.
> We visited *that* town last year.

Chapter 15
DESCRIPTIVE ADJECTIVES

A **descriptive adjective** is a word that characterizes a noun or pronoun. It indicates the quality of that noun or pronoun. As the name implies, it *describes* the noun or pronoun. For example:

The girl is beautiful.

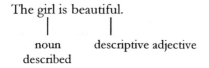

    noun   descriptive adjective
    described

IN ENGLISH
A descriptive adjective does not change form, regardless of the noun or pronoun it modifies.

That is an *excellent* book.
Didn't you think the play was *excellent?*
I have a *blue* shirt.
His pants are *blue.*

Descriptive adjectives are divided into two groups depending on how they accompany the noun they modify.

1. An **attributive adjective** usually precedes (comes before) the noun that it modifies.

That is an *excellent* book.
I have a *blue* shirt.
He is sitting at the *round* table.

2. A **predicate adjective** follows a linking verb such as *be, seem, appear, look, become,* etc.; it refers back to the subject.

The play was *excellent*.
His pants are *blue*.
You look *sad* today.

KWA KISWAHILI

Descriptive adjectives are called **vivumishi vya kueleza**. The singular, *adjective,* is called **kivumishi cha kueleza**. Most descriptive adjectives agree in class with the noun or pronoun that they modify; that is, the prefix of the adjective reflects the class of the word described.

Descriptive adjectives generally use the same prefixes that the nouns themselves use. In the dictionary you will find them listed with out a prefix. Here is a chart illustrating adjectival class agreement using the adjective -**refu**, which means *tall* or *long*, as an example.

CLASS	A. PREFIX	SWAHILI EX.	ENGLISH
1	m-	mtu mrefu	*a tall person*
2	wa-	watu warefu	*tall people*
3	m-	mti mrefu	*a tall tree*
4	mi-	miti mirefu	*tall trees*
5		jina refu	*a long name*
6	ma-	majina marefu	*long names*
7	ki-	kisu kirefu	*a long knife*
8	vi-	visu virefu	*long knives*
9		pati ndefu	*a long party*
10		pati ndefu	*long parties*
11	m-	ulimi mrefu	*a long tongue*
14	m-	uhuru mrefu	*long freedom*
15	ku-	kushona kurefu	*long sewing*
16	pa-	mahali parefu	*a long place*
17	ku-	mahali kurefu	*a long place*
18	mu-	mahali murefu	*a long place*

Your teacher and textbook will explain the exceptions to the general rules embodied in this chart.

Although most adjectives agree with the nouns that they modify using class agreements, there are also a number of adjectives that are invariable, meaning that they never change their form. Here are a few examples.

safi *clean* ⟹ **mtu safi** *clean person*

⟹ **kisu safi** *clean knife*

⟹ **mahali safi** *clean place*

ghali *expensive* ⟹ **tunda ghali** *expensive fruit*

⟹ **kiti ghali** *expensive chair*

⟹ **bei ghali** *expensive price*

When you locate an adjective in the dictionary or glossary, you will know whether or not it is invariable based on whether it is written with a dash before it (such as -**dogo**) or not (such as **bora**). Adjectives written with a dash must always agree with the nouns that they modify, while adjectives written without a dash do not.

As in English, descriptive adjectives in Swahili can be either attributive adjectives or predicate adjectives.

An attributive adjective, called **kivumishi angama** in Swahili, always follows the noun that it modifies.

Hiki ni kitabu <u>kizuri</u>. *This is a good book.*
Nina shati la <u>buluu</u>. *I have a blue shirt.*

A predicate adjective, called **kivumishi arifu** or **kivumishi cha maelezo** in Swahili, follows a linking verb such as **kuwa** (*to be*), **kuonekana** (*to seem, to appear*), **kua** (*to become*), etc.; it refers back to the subject and therefore must agree with it in class.

Mchezo ulikuwa <u>mzuri</u>. *The play/game was good.*
Suruali yake ni <u>nyekundu</u>. *His pants are red.*
Unaonekana <u>mwembemba</u>. *You look skinny.*
Anakuwa <u>mrefu</u>. *He is becoming tall.*

TAKE NOTE

Nouns that refer to people or animals take descriptive adjectives of class 1 if they are singular and class 2 if they are plural, regardless of the class to which the noun itself belongs.

daktari (class 9) $\Rightarrow$ **daktari mzuri**
good doctor
mbwa (class 10) $\Rightarrow$ **mbwa wakali**
vicious dogs

REVIEW

In the sentences below, underline the descriptive adjectives. Circle whether the descriptive adjective is an attributive adjective (A) or a predicate adjective (P).

1. Whose child is this young boy?   A   P

2. I prefer short stories over novels.   A   P

3. Adila is smart.   A   P

4. The tall man is looking at you.   A   P

5. Their house is beautiful.   A   P

Chapter 16
POSSESSIVE ADJECTIVES

A **possessive adjective** is a word that describes a noun by showing who possesses the person or thing referred to by the noun. The owner is called the **possessor**, and the noun modified is called the person or thing **possessed.**

> Whose book is this? It's *his* book.
> - *His* is the possessive adjective.
> - *He* (understood) is the possessor.
> - *Book* is the possessed.

IN ENGLISH
There are eight possessive adjectives.

PERSON	SINGULAR	PLURAL
1st	my	our
2nd	your	your
3rd	his, her, its	their

The possessive adjective refers only to the person who possesses, that is, the possessor.

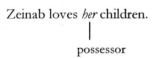

> Zeinab loves *her* children.
>
> possessor

When the 3rd person singular (*his, her, its*) and plural (*their*) are used, there may be two possible meanings.

Ustadhi destroyed *his* car in an accident.
- Ustadhi destroyed his own car.
  OR
- Ustadhi destroyed someone else's car.

Usually the context of the sentence will help you understand the correct meaning; however, when there is a possibility of misunderstanding, the word *own* is added after the possessive adjective.

Ustadhi destroyed *his own* car in an accident.

In this case, and whenever *own* can be added after the possessive adjective, the possessive adjective is called **reflexive**; it "reflects back" to the possessor, which is usually the subject of the sentence or clause.

The family moved into their house.
> (referring to their own house)

If the possessive adjective refers to a possessor other than the subject of the sentence or clause, it is called **non-reflexive.**

The family moved into their house.
> (referring to someone else's house)

KWA KISWAHILI

A possessive adjective is called **kimilikishi**.[7] The plural, *possessive adjectives,* is **vimilikishi**. The possessive adjective for Swahili are as follows:

PERSON	SINGULAR	PLURAL
1st	**-angu** *(my)*	**-etu** *(our)*
2nd	-ako *(your)*	**-enu** *(your pl.)*
3rd	**-ake** *(his, her, its)*	**-ao** *(their)*

Here is a chart illustrating possessive adjectival class agreement using the possessive adjective -**angu**, which means *my*, as an example.

CLASS	POSS. PREFIX	SWAHILI EXAMPLE	ENGLISH TRANSLATION
1	w-	mtoto wangu	*my child*
2	w-	watoto wangu	*my children*
3	w-	mti wangu	*my tree*
4	y-	miti yangu	*my trees*
5	l-	jina langu	*my name*
6	-	majina yangu	*my names*
7	ch-	kiti changu	*my chair*
8	vy	viti vyangu	*my chairs*
9	y-	ndizi yangu	*my banana*
10	z-	ndizi zangu	*my bananas*
11	w-	ulimi wangu	*my tongue*
14	w-	uhuru wangu	*my freedom*
15	kw-	kuandika kwangu	*my writing*
16	p-	nyumbani pangu	*at my house*
17	kw-	nyumbani kwangu	*at my house*[8]
18	mw-	nyumbani mwangu	*in my house*

---

[7] Another Swahili term for the possessive adjective is **kivumishi cha mwenyewe** (Broomfield 68).

[8] The difference between "at my house" in Class 16 and Class 17 is that Class 16 is slightly more specific. Class 17 could indicate not only the house but also the space around it.

The other possessive adjective roots use the same possessive prefixes listed here to form possessive adjectives.

The same prefixes are used to express the possessive preposition *of*, with the root -**a** preceded by the noun possessed and followed by the possessor.

CLASS	SWAHILI EX.	ENGLISH TRANSLATION
1	mtoto wa Juma	*Juma's child*
2	watoto wa Juma	*Juma's children*
3	mti wa Zakia	*Zakia's tree*
4	miti ya Zakia	*Zakia's trees*
5	jina la mwalimu	*the teacher's name*
6	majina ya walimu	*the teachers' names*
7	kiti cha daktari	*the doctor's chair*
8	viti vya daktari	*the doctor's chairs*
9	ndege ya rais	*the president's plane*
10	ndege za rais	*the president's planes*
11	ulimi wa mbwa	*the dog's tongue*
14	uhuru wa nchi	*the country's freedom*
15	kuandika kwa Musa	*Musa's writing*
16	nyumbani pa Sudi	*at Sudi's house*
17	nyumbani kwa Sudi	*at Sudi's house*
18	nyumbani mwa Sudi	*in Sudi's house*

As in English, when the 3rd person singular (-**ake**) and plural (-**ao**) are used, there may be two possible meanings.

> **Ustadhi aliharibu gari lake.** *Ustadhi destroyed his car.*
> - Ustadhi destroyed his own car.
>   OR
> - Ustadhi destroyed someone else's car.

Usually the context of the sentence will help you understand the correct meaning; however, when there is a possibility of misunderstanding, the word -**enyewe** *(himself, herself, itself)* is added after the possessive adjective. Using the possessive prefixes given in the chart above, the adjective -**enyewe** agrees in class with the noun that is the possessor. For example:

Ustadhi aliharibu gari lake mwenyewe.
Ustadhi destroyed his own car.

In this case, and whenever **-enyewe** can be added after the possessive adjective, the possessive adjective is called reflexive (**kimilikishi kinachojirejea** in Swahili); it "reflects back" to the possessor which is usually the subject of the sentence or clause.

Familia walihamia nyumbani kwao.
The family moved into their house.
        (referring to their own house)

If the possessive adjective refers to a possessor other than the subject of the sentence or clause, it is called non-reflexive, or **kimilikishi kisichojirejea** in Swahili.

Familia walihamia nyumbani kwao.
The family moved into their house.
        (referring to someone else's house)

Possessive Contractions
Swahili possessive adjectives can be contracted in a number of ways.

If the noun possessed ends in the vowel -a, it can elide with the four possessive adjectives whose roots begin with the vowel -a (-**angu**, -**ako**, -**ake**, and -**ao**). If this occurs the possessive prefix is dropped. This contraction is most commonly used with nouns that refer to family members (e.g. **mama**, **baba**, **dada**, **kaka**), a number of which end in the vowel -a. Using a contraction does not change the meaning.

> mama yangu ⇒ **mamangu** *my mother*
> mama yake ⇒ **mamake** *his/her mother*
> mama yao ⇒ **mamao** *their mother*

The third person singular possessive, -**ake**, can be contracted with almost any noun that it modifies. When contracted, it keeps the possessive prefix and its last vowel, -**e**, but becomes attached as a suffix to the end of the noun modified. This type of contraction is most commonly used to refer to family members and in poetry.

> mume wake ⇒ **mumewe** *her husband*
> titi lake ⇒ **titile** *her breast*
> bibi yake ⇒ **bibiye** *his/her grandmother*

TAKE NOTE

1. The possessive adjective is not as commonly used in Swahili as it is in English. For example, in English, people often use the possessive adjective to refer to people whom they employ.

> *I saw my doctor today.*
> *Our cleaning lady was ill yesterday.*
> *My seamstress is sewing me a dress.*

In Swahili this is not the case. These three sentences, for example, would not use the possessive adjective.

Nilimwona daktari leo.
I saw a/the doctor today.
Msaidizi aliumwa jana.
The helper was sick yesterday.
Mshonaji ananishonea gauni.
The sewer is sewing me a dress.

When referring to people, possessive adjectives are usually used to refer to family or friends.

Nahitaji kumwuliza mama yangu.
I need to ask my mother.
Rafiki yako ni nani?
Who is your friend?

2. Another way that possessive adjectives in Swahili differ from those in English is that Swahili often uses a plural possessive where English uses the singular possessive. For example, *a house* or *a country* in Swahili is almost always possessed by more than one person.

Most speakers would not use the word **kwangu** (*my*) with the word **nyumbani** (*house*).

Unakaribishwa nyumbani kwetu.
You are invited to our house.

Similarly, most speakers would not use the word **yangu** (*my*) with the word **nchi** (*country*).

Katika nchi yetu, kuna watu wengi.
In our country, there are many people.

3. All nouns take possessive adjectives of the class to which the noun itself belongs, even if they refer to people or animals (which in other circumstances would be considered class 1 and 2 nouns).

mama (class 9) ⇒ **mama yangu** *my mother*
mbwa (class 10) ⇒ **mbwa wetu** *our dogs*

REVIEW

A. Below are a series of English sentences, followed by a Swahili translation in which the possessive adjective or preposition has been left blank. Fill in the Swahili possessive. In the blanks below each pair of sentences, write your answers in both English and Swahili.

1. We bought our car on Vuga Road.
   Tulinunua motokaa _yetu_ **katika mtaa wa Vuga.**

   Possessor: _____

   Noun Possessed: _____

   _____

2. You all bought your cars on Vuga Road.

   Mlinunua motokaa ___zenu___ **katika mtaa wa Vuga.**

   Possessor: _____

   Noun Possessed:

   _____

3. They bought their cars on Vuga Road.

   Walinunua motakaa ___zao___ **katika mtaa wa Vuga.**

   Possessor: _____

   Noun Possessed:

   _____

4. She bought her car on Vuga Road.

   Alinunua motokaa ___yake___ **katika mtaa wa Vuga.**

   Possessor: _____

   Noun Possessed:

   _____

5. I bought my car on Vuga Road.

   Nilinunua motokaa ___yangu___ **katika mtaa wa Vuga.**

   Possessor: _____

   Noun Possessed:

   _____

B.   For each Swahili phrase listed below, list the possible contractions. If no contraction is possible write "none."

1. **dada yake** *his/her sister*

    dadaye   _dadake_

2. **mtoto wao** *their child*

    _____   _____×_____

3. **baba yangu** *my father*

    _____   _babangu_

4. **gari lake** *his vehicle*

    garile   _____×_____

5. **paka wako** *your cat*

    _____   _pakako_

Chapter 17
INTERROGATIVE ADJECTIVES

An **interrogative adjective** is a word that asks a question about a noun. For example:

> *Which* course do you want?
> |
> asks information about the noun *course*

IN ENGLISH

The words *what, which,* and *whose* are called interrogative adjectives when they come before a noun and are used to ask a question about that noun.

> *What* chair do you like to sit in?
> |
>   noun

> *Which* bag is Adila's?
> |
>   noun

> *Whose* house is that?
> |
>   noun

What and *which* are used interchangeably to ask for different kinds of information about a noun:

- the name of a person or thing
  What car did he buy? The Toyota.
  Which countries did they visit? Tanzania, Kenya, and Uganda.

- the kind of person or thing
  What (sort of) dog bit you? A brown and white dog.
  Which (sort of) foods do they like? Rice and meat.

KWA KISWAHILI

Interrogative adjectives are called **vivumishi vya kuuliza.** The singular, *interrogative adjective,* is called **kivumishi cha kuuliza.** There are three types of interrogative adjectives: **gani, -pi,** and **-ngapi.** The one used depends on the type of information being asked about the noun.

Like all Swahili adjectives, the interrogative adjectives always come after the noun they modify.

1. gani?

The interrogative adjective **gani** (*what?*) is an invariable adjective, which means it does not need to agree with the noun it modifies.

Anampenda mvulana gani?
What boy does she like?
Ulinunua kitabu gani?
What book did you buy?

2. -pi?

The interrogative adjective **-pi** (*which?*) must agree in class with the noun it modifies. The prefixes it uses are the same as the verb subject markers (see Chapter 20, *Subject Prefixes*), except in class 1, where the prefix is **yu-**.

Anapenda mvulana yupi?
Which boy does she like?
Ulinunua kitabu kipi.
Which book did you buy?

While **gani** and -**pi** can be used interchangeably like *what* and *which* in English, **gani** is used more often. The interrogative adjective -**pi** is more likely to be used when the possible answers to the question *which?* are understood.

Mtatembelea nchi ipi?
Which country (of the understood options) will you all visit?

3. -ngapi?

The interrogative adjective -**ngapi** (*how many?*) must agree in class with the noun it modifies. The prefixes used are the same as those used for descriptive adjectives (see Chapter 15, *Descriptive Adjectives*). It can only be used with plural nouns.

Tutaalika watu wangapi?
How many people will we invite?
Motakaa ngapi ziliuzwa?
How many cars were sold?

TAKE NOTE

1. Nouns that refer to people or animals take interrogative adjectives of class 1 if they are singular and class 2 if they are plural, regardless of the class to which the noun itself belongs.

    daktari (class 9) ⇒ **daktari yupi?** *which doctor?*
    mbwa (class 10) ⇒ **mbwa wapi?** *which dogs?*

2. The word *what* is not always an interrogative adjective. In the sentence *What are you doing?*, it is an interrogative pronoun. It is important that you distinguish one from the other, because in Swahili a different word is used for the interrogative adjective *what* (**gani?**) and the interrogative pronoun *what* (**nini?**). **Nini** also follows

different rules, which are explained in Chapter 9, *Interrogative Pronouns*.

REVIEW

Circle the interrogative adjective in each of the sentences below. Draw an arrow to the noun each adjective modifies. Circle the interrogative adjective that would be used in Swahili.

1. What cereal do you like to eat?

    gani   -ipi   -ngapi

2. How many times a week to do you exercise?

    gani   -ipi   **-ngapi**

3. Which movie does he want to see?

    gani   -ipi   -ngapi

4. What town do they live in?

    gani   -ipi   -ngapi

5. What page is the teacher reading from?

    gani   -ipi   -ngapi

Chapter 18
DEMONSTRATIVE ADJECTIVES

A **demonstrative adjective** is a word used to point out a noun. It is called demonstrative because it points out (demonstrates) a person or thing. For example:

This boy is handsome.
|
points out the noun *boy*

IN ENGLISH

The demonstrative adjectives are *this* and *that* in the singular and *these* and *those* in the plural. They are a rare example of English adjectives agreeing with the noun they modify: *this* changes to *these* before a plural noun and *that* changes to *those*.

SINGULAR	PLURAL
this picture	*that* picture
that window	*those* windows

The distinction between *this* and *that* can be used to contrast one object with another or to refer to things that are not the same distance away from the speaker. We generally say *this* (or *these*) for a closer object, and *that* (or *those*) for one farther away.

Adija uses two school bags. *This* one is for her books.
|
showing contrast

That one is for her lunch.

|

showing contrast

referring to things at hand

|

These things go in the blue bag. *Those* things go in the red bag.

|

referring to things at a distance

KWA KISWAHILI

There are three types of demonstrative adjectives, which are
called **vionyeshi** in Swahili.   The singular, *demonstrative
adjective*, is called **kionyeshi.** The one used depends on the
distance between the speaker or hearer and the object or
person pointed out, as well as on whether this is the first time
the object or person is being mentioned or a reference to
someone or something that has already been mentioned. All
demonstrative adjectives must agree with the noun they
modify using a system of class agreements.

1.   The first type of demonstrative adjective is equivalent to
     the English demonstratives *this* or *these*. It is used exactly
     as *this* and *these* are used in English.

CLASS	DEM. ADJ.	SWAHILI EX.	ENGLISH TRANSLATION
1	huyu	mtu huyu	*this person*
2	hawa	watu hawa	*these people*
3	huu	mti huu	*this tree*
4	hii	miti hii	*these trees*
5	hili	jina hili	*this name*
6	haya	majina haya	*these names*
7	hiki	kiti hiki	*this chair*
8	hivi	viti hivi	*these chairs*
9	hii	grosari hii	*this gocery store*
10	hizi	grosari hizi	*these grocery stores*
11	huu	ukuta huu	*this wall*
14	huu	uhuru huu	*this freedom*
15	huku	kuandika huku	*this writing*
16	hapa	mahali hapa	*this specific place*
17	huku	mahali huku	*this general place*
18	humu	mahali humu	*this inside place*

While you should try to memorize the demonstrative for each class, you will learn them much faster if you understand how they are formed by studying patterns in the chart above.

All of the demonstratives that mean *this* or *these* begin with the letter *h* and end with the same syllable used as a subject prefix in verbs (see Chapter 20, *Subject Prefixes*). The one exception is in class 1, where the syllable **yu-** is used rather than the subject prefix **a-**. The sound in between the *h* and the subject prefix is always the same as the final vowel.

Here are a few examples of how this demonstrative is formed in different classes. Try to see the pattern for the other classes.

class 1   *h-* + *-u-* + *-yu* = **huyu**
class 5   *h-* + *-i-* + *-li* = **hili**
class 14   *h-* + *-u-* + *-u* = **huu**
class 16   *h-* + *-a-* + *-pa* = **hapa**

2. The second type of demonstrative is equivalent to the
    English demonstratives *that* or *those,* and is used to refer
    to people or things that are distant from the speaker and
    hearer.

CLASS	DEM. ADJ.	SWAHILI EX.	ENGLISH TRANSLATION
1	**yule**	**mtu yule**	*that person over there*
2	**wale**	**watu wale**	*those people over there*
3	**ule**	**mti ule**	*that tree over there*
4	**ile**	**miti ile**	*those trees over there*
5	**lile**	**jina lile**	*that name over there*
6	**yale**	**majina yale**	*those names over there*
7	**kile**	**kiti kile**	*that chair over there*
8	**vile**	**viti vile**	*those chairs over there*
9	**ile**	**grosari ile**	*that grocery over there*
10	**zile**	**grosari zile**	*those groceries over there*
11	**ule**	**ukuta ule**	*that wall over there*

14	**ule**	**uhuru ule**	*that freedom over there*
15	**kule**	**kuandika kule**	*that writing over there*
16	**pale**	**mahali pale**	*that specific place over there*
17	**kule**	**mahali kule**	*that general place over there*
18	**mle**	**mahali mle**	*that inside place over there*

While you should try to memorize the demonstrative for each class, you will learn them much faster if you understand how they are formed by studying patterns in the chart above.

All of the demonstratives that mean *these* or *those objects or people mentioned earlier* begin with the same subject prefixes used with verbs (see Chapter 20, *Subject Prefixes*) and end with the syllable -**le**. The one exception is in class 1, where the syllable **yu**- is used rather than the subject prefix **a**-. Here are a few examples of how this demonstrative is formed in different classes. Try to see the pattern for the other classes.

class 2	wa- + -le	= **wale**
class 4	i- + -le	= **ile**
class 7	ki- + -le	= **kile**
class 18	m- + -le	= **mle**

3. The third type of demonstrative is also equivalent to the English demonstrative *that* or *those*, but it is used to refer to a person or thing that has been previously mentioned.

CLASS	DEM. ADJ.	SWAHILI EX.	ENGLISH TRANSLATION
1	huyo	mtu huyo	*that person mentioned earlier*
2	hao	watu hao	*those people mentioned earlier*
3	huo	mti huo	*that tree mentioned earlier*
4	hiyo	miti hiyo	*those trees mentioned earlier*
5	hiyo	jina hilo	*that name mentioned earlier*
6	hayo	majina hayo	*those names mentioned earlier*
7	hicho	kiti hicho	*that chair mentioned earlier*
8	hivyo	viti hivyo	*those chairs mentioned earlier*
9	hiyo	grosari hiyo	*that grocery mentioned earlier*
10	hizo	grosari hizo	*those groceries mentioned earlier*
11	huo	ukuta huo	*that wall mentioned earlier*
14	huo	uhuru huo	*that freedom mentioned earlier*
15	huko	kuandika huko	*that writing mentioned earlier*
16	hapo	mahali hapo	*that exact place mentioned earlier*
17	huko	mahali huko	*that gen. place mentioned earlier*
18	humo	mahali humo	*that inside place mentioned earlier*

While you should try to memorize the demonstrative for each class, you will learn them much faster if you understand how they are formed by studying patterns in the chart above.

All of the demonstratives that mean *these* or *those objects or people mentioned earlier* follow the pattern of the demonstratives that mean *this* or *these,* except that the final vowel changes to

-o. Here are a few examples of how this demonstrative is formed in different classes. Try to see the pattern for the other classes.

class 1	**huyu**	⇒ **huyo**
class 3	**huu**	⇒ **huo**
class 10	**hizi**	⇒ **hizo**
class 17	**huku**	⇒ **huko**

Note that in classes 4, 7, 8, and 9 the vowel change (from -**i** to -**o**) results in a sound change in the preceding consonant(s).

class 4 & 9	**hii**	⇒ **hiyo**
class 7	**hiki**	⇒ **hicho**
class 8	**hivi**	⇒ **hivyo**

1. Unlike most Swahili adjectives, two of the demonstrative adjectives—the one that means *this* or *that* and the one that refers to objects or people mentioned previously—can be used either before or after the noun without changing the meaning.

    huyu mtu OR **mtu huyu**   *this person*
    hili jina OR **jina hili**   *this name*

2. When referring to a location (i.e. class 16, 17 or 18), all of the demonstrative adjectives almost always come before the noun.

hapa nyumbani	*right here at this home*
pale nyumbani	*over there at that house*
hapo nyumbani	*at that specific house mentioned earlier*
huku Tanzania	*here in Tanzania*
kule Tanzania	*(over there) in Tanzania*
huko Tanzania	*in Tanzania (previously mentioned)*
humu mfukoni	*in this bag*
mle mfukoni	*in that bag over there*
humo mfukoni	*in that bag I mentioned earlier*

If the demonstrative used to refer to *that* or *those* objects or people at a distance is placed before the noun it approximates, the English article *the* and refers to someone or something mentioned earlier.

Mwalimu alienda shuleni. Huko shuleni alimwona mwanafunzi. <u>Yule mwanafunzi</u> alianza kulia kwa sababu alisahau zoezi lake la nyumbani.	*A teacher went to school. At school she saw a student. <u>The student</u> began to cry because she forgot her homework.*

REVIEW

For the English sentences, circle the demonstrative adjective that would be used in Swahili. For the Swahili sentences, circle the demonstrative adjectives. Draw an arrow to the noun each adjective modifies. In some cases, the noun may be understood but not explicated stated.

1. Do you like this shirt?

    (hii)   ile   hiyo

2. No, I prefer that one.

    hii   (ile)   hiyo

3. What about these shoes?

    (hivi)   vile   hivyo

4. Yes, those are really nice.

    hivi   (vile)   hivyo

5. Where did you get the hat you had on yesterday?

    hii   ile   (hiyo)

6. **Nilinunua kofia hiyo pale dukani.**
    (*I bought that hat at that store over there.*)

7. **Tuende hapo dukani.** (*Let's go to that store.*)

8. **Subiri kidogo; nahitaji kulipia suruali hizi.**
    (*Wait a little; I need to pay for these pants.*)

9. **Usinunue zile; hizi ni bora.**
    (*Don't buy those; these are better.*)

10. **Lakini hizi zinanifaa kuliko hizo.**
    (*But these fit me better than those.*)

Chapter 19
SUBJECTS

The **subject** of a sentence is the person, object, or idea being described. When you wish to find the subject of a sentence, identify the verb and then ask *who?* or *what?* before the verb. The answer will be the subject. For example:

The *girl* slept in the room.
|
subject of the verb *slept*

The *key* broke.
|
subject of the verb *broke*

IN ENGLISH
The subject of the sentence performs the action of a verb or is acted upon by a passive verb. You will learn more about passive verbs in Chapters 41 (Verb Extensions) and 44 (Active and Passive Voice). The subject is a noun, a pronoun or a phrase that is used as a noun.

The dog wagged its tail.
- What wagged its tail? The dog.
- *The dog* is a noun, which functions as the subject.

She studies Swahili and Arabic.
- Who studies Swahili and Arabic? She.
- *She* is a pronoun, which functions as the subject.

Walking to Iringa took two hours.
- What took two hours? Walking to Iringa.
- *Walking to Iringa* is a phrase used as a noun that functions as the subject.

Train yourself to ask *who?* or *what?* to find the subject. Never assume that the first word in the sentence is the subject. Subjects can occur in many different places in a sentence.

While shopping, *Salma* lost her bag.
Do *you* like pilau?
"Why?" asked *Mariamu.*

Some sentences have more than one main verb; you need to find the subject of each verb.

Sudi watched television and *Zuhura* read a book.
- *Sudi* is the subject of the first verb, *watched.*
- *Zuhura* is the subject of the second verb, *read.*

A singular subject takes a singular verb; a plural subject takes a plural verb. The verb must agree with its subject in number. Noun classes are explained in Chapter 3.

KWA KISWAHILI

The subject of a sentence is called **mtenda** or **kiima**. The plural, *subjects*, is called **watenda** or **viina**. Subjects function in the same way in Swahili as they do in English. It is particularly important that you recognize the subject of the sentence in Swahili so that you will make the subject marker of the verb agree with the noun class of the subject.

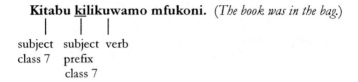

Kitabu <u>ki</u>likuwamo mfukoni. *(The book was in the bag.)*

subject   subject   verb
class 7   prefix
           class 7

TAKE NOTE

In both English and Swahili it is very important to recognize the subject of each verb. You must make sure that each verb agrees with its subject; that is, you must use a class 1 subject marker when a class 1 noun is the subject, and a class 10 subject marker when a class 10 noun is the subject. You will learn more about subject markers in the next chapter.

REVIEW

Underline the subject(s) in each of these sentences.

1. The tall trees will fall over if it is too windy.

2. Drinking tea in the morning is quite pleasant.

3. As I walked by the car, the driver waved at me.

4. After passing through Zanzibar, the storm hit Pemba.

5. Pilau is made with rice, vegetables and spices.

CHAPTER 20
SUBJECT PREFIXES

While English does not have subject prefixes (also called subject markers), they are extremely important in Swahili. The **subject prefix** of a verb indicates the class of its subject, which will also indicate whether the noun of the subject is singular or plural.

IN ENGLISH
There are no subject prefixes. Instead, English uses nouns and personal pronouns (*he, she, it,* and *they*) to indicate the subject of a sentence.

> *John* is playing ball.
> |
> subject (noun)

> *He* will be home at 6 o'clock.
> |
> subject (personal pronoun)

KWA KISWAHILI
Each noun class and personal pronoun has its own subject prefix, called **kiambishi awali**. In the plural it is **viambishi awali**. The subject prefix is the same for all the tenses, except for some of the personal pronouns, which have different prefixes for the -**a**- tense. (You will learn more about verb tenses in the next chapter.) The subject prefix is attached to the verb. It always comes first, followed by the tense and then the verb in the dictionary form.

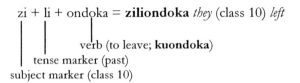

As explained in Chapter 21(Introduction to Verbs & Verb Tenses), Swahili is called an **agglutinating language** because it agglutinates (i.e. sticks together) a lot of meaningful sound segments to form a word that could be considered a phrase or even a sentence in English.

Personal Pronouns
Each personal pronoun – *I, you* (singular), *he/she, we, you* (plural), and *they* – has a subject prefix. Personal pronouns are explained in Chapter 7.

PERSONAL PRONOUN **Kiwakilishi nomino cha mtu**	SUBJECT MARKER **Kiambishi awali**	SUBJECT MARKER (PRESENT) **Kiambishi awali cha wakati uliopo**
mimi (*I*)	**Ni-**	**na-**
wewe (*you singular*)	**u-**	**wa-**
yeye (*he or she*)	**a-**	**a-**
sisi (*we*)	**Tu-**	**twa-**
ninyi (*you plural*)	**m-**	**mwa-**
wao (*they*)	**wa-**	**wa-**

Mimi ninaenda kwa daktari. *I am going to the doctor.*

subject marker -1st person singular

Watoto <u>wa</u>nacheza. *The children are playing.*

subject marker - 3rd person plural

Ninyi <u>m</u>tapewa zawadi. *You all will be given gifts.*

subject marker - 2nd person plural

CLASS 1
The subject marker for class 1 is the same as the third person singular (he or she), **a-**. It is the same for all tenses of the verb.

Mtu <u>a</u>napika. *The person is cooking.*

CLASS 2
The subject marker for class 2 is the same as the third person plural (they), **wa-**. It is the same for all tenses of the verb.

Watu <u>wa</u>napika. *People are cooking.*

CLASS 3
The subject marker for class 3 is **u-**. It is the same for all tenses of the verb.

Mti <u>u</u>naanguka chini. *The tree is falling down.*

CLASS 4
The subject marker for class 4 is **i-**. It is the same for all tenses of the verb.

Miti <u>i</u>naanguka chini. *The trees are falling down.*

CLASS 5

The subject marker for class 5 is **li-**. It is the same for all tenses of the verb.

Jengo lilijengwa mwaka huu.
The building was built this year.

CLASS 6

The subject marker for class 6 is **ya-**. It is the same for all tenses of the verb.

Majengo yalijengwa mwaka huu.
The buildings were built this year.

CLASS 7

The subject marker for class 7 is **ki-**. This prefix is easy to remember because it is the same as the nominal prefix for nouns of class 7, like **kisu** or **kipindi**. It is the same for all tenses of the verb.

Kiswahili kinasemwa kule Afrika ya Mashariki.
Swahili is spoken in East Africa.

CLASS 8

The subject marker for class 8 is **vi-**. This prefix is easy to remember because it is the same as the nominal prefix for nouns of class 8, like **visu** or **vipindi**. It is the same for all tenses of the verb.

Visiwa vinapata watalii wengi.
The islands get many tourists.

CLASS 9

The subject marker for class 9 is **i-**. It is the same for all tenses of the verb.

Safari <u>i</u>lienda vizuri. *The trip went well.*

CLASS 10

The subject marker for class 10 is **zi-**. It is the same for all tenses of the verb.

Safari <u>zi</u>lienda vizuri. *The trips went well.*

CLASS 11

The subject marker for class 11 is **u-**. This prefix is easy to remember because it is the same as the nominal prefix for nouns of class 11, like **ubao** or **ufunguo**. It is the same for all tenses of the verb.

Ulimi wangu <u>u</u>nauma. *My tongue hurts.*

CLASS 14

The subject marker for class 14 is **u-**. This prefix is easy to remember because it is the same as the nominal prefix for nouns of class 14, like **umoja** or **uzima**. It is the same for all tenses of the verb.

Uhuru <u>u</u>lipatikana miaka ya sitini.
Freedom was achieved in the 1960s.

CLASS 15

The subject marker for class 15 is **ku-**. This prefix is easy to remember because it is the same as the infinitive prefix for nouns of class 15, like **kulinda** or **kuchukua**. It is the same for all tenses of the verb.

Kushona <u>ku</u>nanifurahisha.
Sewing makes me happy.

CLASS 16

The subject marker for class 16 is **pa-**. It is the same for all tenses of the verb.

Nyumbani <u>pa</u>likuwa na watu wengi.
There were many people in the house.
(literally: *At the house the place had many people.*)

CLASS 17

The subject marker for class 17 is **ku-**. It is the same for all tenses of the verb.

Mjini <u>ku</u>takuwa na hali ya hewa nzuri.
In the city there will be good weather.
(literally: *In the city the place will have good weather.*)

CLASS 18

The subject marker for class 18 is **m-**, **mu-** or **mw-**.

Mfukoni <u>mu</u>na matofaa.
In the bag there are apples.
(literally: *In the bag the place has apples.*)

SUBJECT PREFIXES WITHOUT NOUNS
While a subject prefix always agrees in class with the subject of the sentence, it also allows you to leave out the noun of the subject if both the speaker and the listener understand it.

Instead of saying:	**You could simply say:**
Mimi <u>ni</u>lienda dukani. *I went to the store.*	**<u>Ni</u>lienda dukani.** *I went to the store.*
Watoto walienda dukani. *The children went to the store.*	**Walienda dukani.** *They went to the store.* (*Children* is understood.)
Ndizi zitauzwa. *The bananas will be sold.*	**Zitauzwa.** *They will be sold.* (*Bananas* is understood.)

TAKE NOTE

In Chapter 3 (*Noun Class*) you learned that sometimes you will need to look for clues in the sentence to know whether a noun is singular or plural. Here you have learned about subject prefixes, one example of this kind of grammatical clue. Recognizing the subject marker will help you to figure out in what class the noun of the subject belongs, including whether it is singular or plural.

For example, if you see or hear a sentence where the subject marker on the verb is **ya-**, you will know that the subject is a class 6 noun.

Matunda yalikatwa.
The fruit was cut.

If you see or hear a sentence where the subject marker on the verb is **i-**, you will know that the subject is either a class 4 or a class 9 noun. Looking at the noun itself will help you choose between these two possibilities.

Mikutano ilivunjika.
The meetings were cancelled.

Since you already know that class 4 nouns begin with **mi-**, in this case you can tell that the noun is a class 4 noun.

Safari ilivunjika
The trip was cancelled.

Since the noun has no nominal prefix, you can tell that **safari** is a class 9 noun.

REVIEW

Circle the subject prefix of each verb, and draw a line from it to the subject with which it agrees. (In some cases the subject may be understood but not stated.) Identify the noun class of each subject prefix. You should be able to do this even if you don't know what these words mean. If you find this difficult you might need to reread Chapter 3 (Noun Class).

1. **Wewe utaenda shuleni lini?** Class _____

2. **Vitabu vilinunuliwa jana.** Class _____

3. **Maembe yananuka.** Class_____

4. **Anapenda kuogolea.** Class _____

5. **Vijana watagombana.** Class _____

6. **Jiwe linatupwa.** Class _____

7. **Muhogo uliuzwa sokoni.** Class _____

8. **Kulia kwake kunanisikitisha.** Class _____

9. **Sherehe zitaanza wiki ijayo.** Class _____

10. **Utoto wake unaonekana wazi.** Class _____

VERBS

Chapter 21
INTRODUCTION TO VERBS AND VERB TENSES

A **verb** is a word that signifies an action, occurrence, state of being, or condition. The action can be bodily, as in such verbs as *cry, laugh, sew,* or *repair,* or mental, as in such verbs as *wonder, desire, plan, love.* Verbs such as *be* and *become* express a state or condition rather than an action.

The verb is at the grammatical center of a sentence; you usually cannot express a complete thought without a verb.

To train yourself to recognize verbs, read the following paragraph where the verbs are in italics.

> Zainab and her family *are* Muslims. Every day they *wake* at dawn *to pray.* After breakfast she *dresses* her children, who *get ready to go* to school. During the day she *cooks* and *cleans,* but in the evenings Zainab *teaches* Koranic lessons to other women, something she *enjoys doing* because it *gives* her some time away from *taking* care of her family.

The **tense** of a verb specifies when the action of the verb takes place: in the present, in the past, or in the future.

| **present** I go | **past** I went | **future** I will go |

As the above examples demonstrate, you can indicate when the action of the verb takes place by putting the verb in a different tense without giving any additional information such as *I go now* or *I went yesterday* or *I will go tomorrow.*

IN ENGLISH
There are two kinds of verbs depending on whether the verb can take a direct object: transitive verbs and intransitive verbs. A **transitive verb** is one that takes a direct object. You will learn more about direct objects in Chapter 35. In some dictionaries, a transitive verb is indicated by the abbreviation *v.t.* (verb transitive).

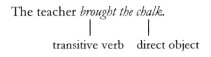

The teacher *brought the chalk.*
transitive verb   direct object

The traditional healer *sells medicine.*
transitive verb   direct object

An **intransitive verb** is a verb that does not take a direct object. Some dictionaries indicate an intransitive verb with the abbreviation *v.i.* (verb intransitive).

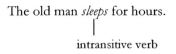

The old man *sleeps* for hours.
intransitive verb

My father *runs* every day in the morning.
intransitive verb

There are six main **tenses** in English.

present	I go	**present perfect**	I have gone
past	I went	**past perfect**	I had gone
future	I will go	**future perfect**	I will have gone

The listing of the forms of a verb in all six tenses is called a **synopsis.** Above is a synopsis of the verb *go* in the first person singular. These tenses are discussed individually in Chapters 22-29. There are also more complex tenses that can be created by combining the main tenses; these will be explained in Chapter 43, Compound Tenses.

KWA KISWAHILI
Verbs are called **vitenzi**, and they are identified in the same way as in English. Transitive verbs are called **vitenzi elekezi.** Intransitive verbs are **vitenzi visoelekezi.** If you are memorizing the definitions of Swahili verbs, be sure to note whether the word is transitive or intransitive. Conjugated Swahili verbs have at least three parts: the subject marker (see Chapter 20), the tense marker (see Chapters 21-44), and the dictionary form.

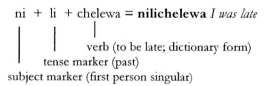

ni + li + chelewa = **nilichelewa** *I was late*

verb (to be late; dictionary form)
tense marker (past)
subject marker (first person singular)

Swahili is called an agglutinative language[9] because it agglutinates (i.e. sticks together) a lot of meaningful sound

---

[9] "Morphology: Morphological Types of Languages," *Language Files,* Monica Crabtree and Joyce Powers, compilers (Columbus: Ohio State U.P., 1991): 159. Some linguists, however, consider Swahili a "parasynthetic language," "one that allows multiple prefixes and suffixes appended to a verbal and/or nominal root" (John Mtembezi Inniss, personal communication, 4 July 2000).

segments to form a word that would be considered a phrase or even a sentence in English.   The process is called **agglutination** or **uambishaji.**

Tenses are called **nyakati** (or **wakati** in the singular) or **tensi.** There are five main tenses in Swahili.

present progressive *wakati uliopo unaoendelea*	**ninaenda** *or* **naenda**	*I am going*
simple present *wakati uliopo sahili*	**ninaenda** *or* **naenda**	*I go*
present perfect *wakati uliopo timilifu*	**nimeenda**	*I have gone*
past *wakati uliopita*	**nilienda**	*I went*
future *wakati ujao*	**nitaenda**	*I will go*

The listing of the forms of the verb in all five tenses is called a **muhtasari** (*summary*).[10]   These tenses are discussed individually in Chapters 22-29.   There are also more complex tenses that can be created by combining the main tenses; these will be explained in Chapter 43, *Compound Tenses.*

---

[10] The word **ufupisho** (*shortening*) or **kidokezo** (*hint or suggestion*) can also be used to express the idea of a *synopsis.* See *TUKI English-Swahili Dictionary* (Dar es Salaam: TUKI, 1996).

REVIEW

A. Underline the verbs in the sentences below.   Circle whether the verb is transitive (V.T.) or intransitive (V.I.).

1. Juma loves his wife.	V.T.	V.I.
2. The book was on the table.	V.T.	V.I.
3. The old man spit when he saw it.	V.T.	V.I.
4. What do you want to do today?	V.T.	V.I.
5. The president will be travelling.	V.T.	V.I.

B. Write a synopsis in the second person singular (**-u-**) for the Swahili verb **kupenda** *(to like)*.

Present Progressive _____
Simple Present _____
Present Perfect _____
Past _____
Future _____

Chapter 22
PRESENT

There are two forms of the verb that indicate the present tense, although they have slightly different meanings.

simple present	Laila *reads* the book.
present progressive	Laila *is reading* the book.

The **simple present** indicates that the action is habitual or occurs regularly. It is used to express a statement of fact.

> I *walk* to the shore.

The **present progressive** indicates that the action is going on at the time when the speaker is speaking.

> I *am walking* to the shore.

IN ENGLISH

As you saw in Chapter 21 (Introduction to Verbs and Verb Tenses), there are three forms of the verb that indicate the present tense, although they have slightly different meanings.

simple present	Laila *reads* the book.
present progressive	Laila *is reading* the book.
present emphatic	Laila *does read* the book.

Combining the verb to be in the present tense with a gerund, or verbal noun, forms the present progressive. You learned about verbal nouns in Chapter 4, and you will learn about the verb *to be* in Chapter 30.

In addition to the simple present and present progressive tenses, English also has the present emphatic tense.

present emphatic   Laila *does read* the book.

To ask questions, you must use the progressive or emphatic form.

> *Is* Laila *reading* the booking?
> *Does* Laila *read* the book?

KWA KISWAHILI

There are also two forms of the verb that indicate the present tense. Both forms can be used to express the present progressive and the simple present tenses. Their usage and precise meaning depend on context, dialect, and personal preference.

present progressive   Laila *is reading* the book
                                 └────────┘
                                 anasoma or *asoma*

simple present   Laila *reads* the book.
                                       │
                                 anasoma or *asoma*

habitual present　　　Laila *usually reads* the book.

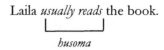

husoma

In Swahili the present progressive is called **wakati uliopo unaoendelea**. It is expressed with either of the tense markers -a- or -na-. While the subject marker changes depending on the class of the subject, the tense marker stays the same as long as the verb remains in the present progressive tense.

In Swahili the simple present is called **wakati uliopo sahili**. It can also be expressed with either of the tense markers -a- or -na-. Both are explained in greater detail below.

In Swahili the habitual present tense is called **wakati uliopa wa kawaida**. It is expressed without a tense marker and with the subject marker **hu-**. It is explained in greater detail below.

THE -A- TENSE

Note how the subject markers combine with the -a- tense marker; their sounds merge to create slightly different forms.

ni + -a- = **n<u>a</u>sogea**　　　*I am moving*
　　　　　　　　　　　　　first person singular

u + -a- = **w<u>a</u>sogea**　　　*you are moving*
　　　　　　　　　　　　　second person singular

a + -a- = **<u>a</u>sogea**　　　*she/ he is moving*
　　　　　　　　　　　　　third person singular (C1)

tu + -a- = **tw<u>a</u>sogea**　　　*we move*
　　　　　　　　　　　　　first person plural

m + -a- = **m<u>wa</u>sogea**   *you all are moving*
                                    second person plural
wa + -a- = **w<u>a</u>sogea**   *they are moving*
                                    third person plural (C2)

Although the translations given here are present progressive,
note that all six of these forms could also express the simple
present tense, depending on context.

As you can see, the -**a**- tense marker is only used with the
personal subject markers, including class 1 and 2. The other
classes (i.e. 3-18) always use the -**na**- tense marker, whether
the tense is simple present or present progressive. You will
need to decide from context whether the meaning is simple
present or present progressive.

Gari la moshi linakwenda kila siku.
The train goes every day.
Sasa hivi gari la moshi linakwenda mjini.
Right now the train is going to town.

To conjugate a Swahili verb with the -**a**- tense marker, start
with the infinitive.

kulinda   *to guard*

For verbs with a dictionary form that is more than one
syllable long, drop the infinitive prefix **ku**-, which leaves you
with the dictionary form.

linda   *to guard*

To this form add the subject marker that agrees with your subject and the tense marker *-a-*.

tu + a + linda = **twalinda** *we guard* or *we are guarding*

      │   │   │
      │   │   verb (to guard; dictionary form)
      │   tense marker
    subject marker (first person plural)

This process works the same way when the dictionary form has only one syllable.

    kula   *to eat* (infinitive)   **-la**   *to eat* (dictionary form)

wa + a + la = **wala** *they eat* or *they are eating*

     │   │   │
     │   │   verb (to eat; dictionary form)
     │   tense marker
    subject marker (third person plural)

THE -NA- TENSE

Here is the verb **kusogea** (*to move*) conjugated using the -na- tense.

ni<u>na</u>sogea	*I am moving*	
	first person singular	
a<u>na</u>sogea	*she/he is moving*	
	third person singular	
m<u>na</u>sogea	*you all are moving*	
	second person plural	
li<u>na</u>sogea	*it is moving*	
	class 5	
u<u>na</u>sogea	*it is moving*	
	class 11 or 14	

Although the translations given here are present progressive, note that all six of these forms could also express the simple present tense, depending on context.

To conjugate a Swahili verb in the -na- tense, start with the infinitive.

kulinda   *to guard*

For verbs with a dictionary form that is more than one syllable long, drop the infinitive prefix **ku-**, which leaves you with the dictionary form.

linda   *to guard*

To this form, add the subject marker that agrees with your subject and the tense marker *-na-*.

tu + na + linda = **tunalinda** *we are guarding* or *we guard*

verb (to guard; dictionary form)
tense marker
subject marker (first person plural)

This process works slightly differently if the dictionary form has only one syllable.

kula   *to eat* (infinitive)   **-la**   *to eat* (dictionary form)

For verbs with only one syllable in the dictionary form, keep the infinitive prefix **ku-** when you add the subject marker and the -**na**- tense marker.

wa + na + kula = **wanakula** *they are eating* or *they eat*

```
 |      |      |
 |      |      verb (to eat; infinitive)
 |      tense marker
subject marker (third person plural)
```

THE PRESENT HABITUAL TENSE
This tense is used to indicate habitual or customary action. It does not use a tense marker or the usual subject markers. Instead the prefix **hu-** is used for all the noun classes. Unless the subject is clear, the subject is indicated by an independent pronoun or other noun subject.

>**Mimi <u>husoma</u> kila siku.**
>*I <u>usually study</u> everyday.*
>**Juma <u>hututembelea</u> kila wikendi.**
>*Juma <u>usually visits</u> us every weekend.*

The *hu-* prefix always comes before the dictionary form of the word. With monosyllabic verbs, therefore, the infinitive prefix **ku-** is dropped.

>**kula** *to eat*
>**Mariam <u>hula</u> ndizi.**
>*Mariamu <u>usually eats</u> bananas.*

TAKE NOTE

There is no emphatic form of the verb in Swahili. If you want to ask a question in the present tense, you must use the simple present or the present progressive, but turn the sentence into a question. You will learn more about asking questions in Chapter 50 (*Declarative and Interrogative Sentences*).

Some verbs in the present progressive tense in Swahili will be translated into the simple present in English.

kufurahi *to be happy* *The farmer is happy.*[11]	**Mkulima anafurahi**. (literally: *The farmer is being happy.*)

As you can see, the literal translation doesn't sound right in English. You should be able to use the context and the word's meaning to decide which tense to use when translating.

---

[11] "*He is happy*" could also be expressed with the perfect tense, by saying "amefurahi."

REVIEW

Below you will find English sentences translated into Swahili with the conjugated Swahili verb missing. Given the infinitive of the verb, conjugate the verb in the present tense to fill in the blanks.

1. The girls are carrying water. (***kubeba*** = *to carry*)

   Wasichana _____ maji.

2. Sudi's family is moving to Dar es Salaam.
   (***kuhamia*** = *to move to*)

   Familia ya Sudi _____ Dar es Salaam.

3. The trees are growing quickly. (***kukua*** = *to grow*)

   Miti _____ kwa haraka.

4. The European is visiting East Africa.
   (***kutembelea*** = *to visit*)

   Mzungu _____ Afrika ya Mashariki.

5. His eye is looking at those buildings.
   (***kuangalia*** = *to look at*)

   Jicho lake _____ majengo hayo.

6. What time do you usually wake up?

    (*kuamka* = *to wake up*)

    Wewe _____ saa ngapi?

7. What do they usually do during vacation?

    (*kufanya* = *to do*)

    Wao _____ nini wakati wa likizo?

Chapter 23
NEGATIVE PRESENT

To negate a verb is to make it negative. An **affirmative** verb is one that is not negated.

> I *am* a student.   He *wants* to be a teacher.
> They would prefer *to go* on the weekend.

A **negative** verb is one that is negated.

> I am *not* a student.
> He does *not* want to be a teacher.
> They would prefer *not* to go on the weekend.

Like all verbs, a present tense verb can be negated.

IN ENGLISH
The present progressive and the simple present tenses each have their own rules for forming the negative.

The present progressive tense is made negative by adding *not* after the auxiliary verb *to be* and before the main verb. You will learn about negating the verb *to be* in Chapter 30.

> The doctor is working in his office.
> The doctor is *not* working in his office.
> | |
> the verb *to be*   the main verb

The simple present tense is made negative by adding *do* or *does* + *not* + the dictionary form of the main verb.

> The doctor works in his office.
> The doctor *does not* work in his office.

Often *do* or *does* is contracted with *not*.

> do not ⇒ don't   Doctors *don't* work.
> does not ⇒ doesn't   A doctor *doesn't* work.

KWA KISWAHILI

The present negative is called **wakati uliopo kanusho**. The -a- tense and the -**na**- tense form the negative in the same way.

> **anasoma** *(she is studying)* ⇒ **hasomi** *(she isn't studying)*

> **asoma** *(she studies)* ⇒ **hasomi** *(she doesn't study)*

You will need to examine the context in order to decide whether a negative present verb suggests a present progressive or simple present tense.

The present tense is made negative by adding the negative prefix **ha**- before the subject marker. After the subject marker, there is no tense marker. The dictionary form of the verb is used, but its ending changes from -**a** to the negative suffix -**i**.

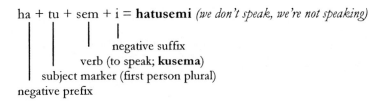

ha + tu + sem + i = **hatusemi** *(we don't speak, we're not speaking)*

negative suffix
verb (to speak; **kusema**)
subject marker (first person plural)
negative prefix

If the dictionary form of the verb ends in a vowel other than -**a**, its ending does not change.

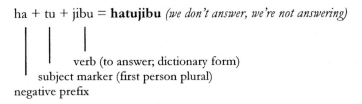

ha + tu + jibu = **hatujibu** *(we don't answer, we're not answering)*

verb (to answer; dictionary form)
subject marker (first person plural)
negative prefix

The only subject for which this process works differently is the first person singular (I). In that case, instead of adding the negative prefix **ha-**, change the subject marker **ni-** to **si-**.

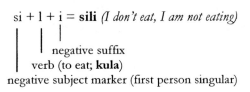

si + l + i = **sili** *(I don't eat, I am not eating)*

negative suffix
verb (to eat; **kula**)
negative subject marker (first person singular)

REVIEW

A. Rewrite the following sentences, putting each verb into the present negative tense.

1. The trees are being cut down.

    _____

2. Those houses are being built.

    _____

3. I think of you as a nice person.

    _____

B. Conjugate the verb **kupenda** (*to love*) in the negative present tense.

I don't love   _____
you don't love   _____
s/he doesn't love   _____
we don't love   _____
you all don't love   _____
they don't love   _____

Chapter 24
PAST

The past tense is used to express an action that occurred in the past. For example:

I *went* to the store yesterday.

|

past tense of the verb *to go*

IN ENGLISH

There are several verb forms that indicate that the action occurred in the past.

simple past	I walked
past progressive	I was walking
past emphatic	I did walk
perfect	I have walked
past perfect	I had walked
past perfect progressive	I had been walking

The simple past is called "simple" because it is a **simple tense**; in other words, it consists of one word (*walked* in the example above). The other past tenses are called **verb phrases** or **compound verbs**; in other words, they consist of more than one word, an auxiliary plus a main verb.

This chapter focuses on the simple past tense. Auxiliary verbs are explained in Chapter 33 and compound tenses in Chapter 43.

To form the simple past tense of regular verbs, adding the suffix *-ed* to the dictionary form of the verb forms the past tense.

to answer	I *answered* his question.
to borrow	They *borrowed* her bicycle.

Irregular verbs, however, change their form dramatically in the past tense. These are just a few examples:

to bring	December *brought* snow and freezing rain.
to fall	The tree *fell* on the house.
to cling	The baby *clung* to her mother.

KWA KISWAHILI

There are several tenses that correspond to the six English tenses listed above.

SIMPLE PAST:
Nilikimbia
I ran

PAST PROGRESSIVE:
Nilikuwa nikikimbia
I was running

PERFECT:
Nimekimbia
I have run

PAST PERFECT:
Nilikuwa nimekimbia
I had run

PAST PERFECT PROGRESSIVE:
Nilikuwa nimekuwa nikikimbia
I had been running

Note that there is no past emphatic tense in Swahili. There is however, an additional form of the past tense that exists in Swahili but not in English. The **-ka-** tense describes an action that follows another action. It is described in greater detail below.

The simple past tense and the perfect tense are called "simple" because they are **simple tenses**; in other words, they consists of one word (*nilitembea* and *nimetembea* in the examples above). The other past tenses are called **verb phrases** or **compound tenses**; in other words, they consist of more than one word, an auxiliary plus a main verb. This chapter focuses on the simple past tense. You will learn more about the perfect tense in Chapter 26, about auxiliary verbs in Chapter 33, and about compound tenses in Chapter 43.

THE SIMPLE PAST TENSE

The simple past tense is called **wakati uliopita**. Its tense marker is the morpheme -**li**-, which occurs after the subject marker and before the verb. The form of the past tense is the same for every subject, including all the noun classes.

For monosyllabic verbs, use the verbal noun form of the verb.

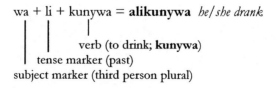

wa + li + kunywa = **alikunywa** *he/she drank*
verb (to drink; **kunywa**)
tense marker (past)
subject marker (third person plural)

For verbs with more than one syllable, use the dictionary form of the verb.

```
u + li + taka = ulitaka  you wanted
|    |    |
|    |    verb (to want; dictionary form)
|    tense marker (past)
subject marker (second person singular)
```

THE -KA- TENSE

This tense is used to indicate a sequence of events. In a sequence of two verbs, the action of the verb marked by -ka- occurred after the time of the verb preceding it. Note that the verb itself incorporates the sense of both the conjunction *and* and the adverb *then*.

Nilifika nyumbani <u>nikamwona</u>.
I arrived at home <u>and (then) saw him</u>.

The morpheme -ka- occurs after the subject marker and before the dictionary form of verb. Monosyllabic verbs, therefore, drop the infinitive prefix **ku-**. The form of the -ka- tense is the same for every subject marker, including all the noun classes.

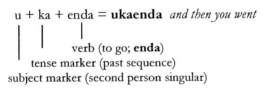

```
u + ka + enda = ukaenda  and then you went
|    |     |
|    |     verb (to go; enda)
|    tense marker (past sequence)
subject marker (second person singular)
```

REVIEW

A. Change the following sentences from present tense to past tense.

1.   I want to go to the movies.

_____

2.   The doctor is coming to dinner.

_____

3.   His grandmother breaks her hip.

_____

4.   **Ndizi zinapikwa.** *(The bananas are being cooked.)*

_____

5.   **Majina yao yanatajwa.** *(Their names are being stated.)*

_____

B. Translate the following sentences.

1.   *I went to the market and bought oranges.*

_____

2.   *He said hello and then left.*

_____

3.   **Ulienda shuleni ukafanya nini?**

_____

4.   **Walinunua baisikeli wakasafiri.**

_____

5.   **Tulipika pilau tukala.**

_____

Chapter 25
NEGATIVE PAST

Like all verbs, a past tense verb can be negated. For example:

I *did not go* to the store last week.

past tense negative of the verb *to go*

IN ENGLISH
The past tense is made negative by putting *did* + *not* before the dictionary form of the verb.

> You all *did not go* to the mosque.
> The children *did not like* to eat chicken.

Sometimes *did* and *not* are contracted.

> you did not ⟹ you didn't

KWA KISWAHILI
The negative past tense is called **wakati uliopita kanusho**. It is formed with the negative prefix **ha-** + the subject marker + the negative tense marker -**ku-** + the dictionary form of the verb.

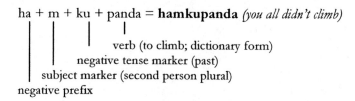

ha + m + ku + panda = **hamkupanda** *(you all didn't climb)*

      verb (to climb; dictionary form)
    negative tense marker (past)
  subject marker (second person plural)
negative prefix

Verbs with a second person singular subject (you) or a third person singular subject (he or she) form the past negative in the same way, but the negative prefix *ha-* combines with the *a-* or *u-* sound of the subject markers to create slightly different results.

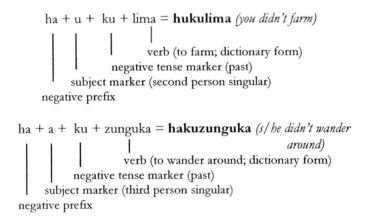

ha + u + ku + lima = **hukulima** *(you didn't farm)*

> verb (to farm; dictionary form)
> negative tense marker (past)
> subject marker (second person singular)
> negative prefix

ha + a + ku + zunguka = **hakuzunguka** *(s/ he didn't wander around)*

> verb (to wander around; dictionary form)
> negative tense marker (past)
> subject marker (third person singular)
> negative prefix

The only subject that forms the past negative differently is the first person singular (I). Instead of adding the negative prefix **ha-**, the first person singular uses the negative subject marker **si-** in place of its positive singular marker **ni-**.

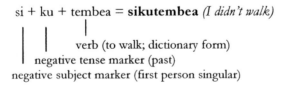

si + ku + tembea = **sikutembea** *(I didn't walk)*

> verb (to walk; dictionary form)
> negative tense marker (past)
> negative subject marker (first person singular)

REVIEW

Rewrite the following sentences using the negative past tense.

1. The books were sold yesterday.

_____

2. The teacher wrote on the blackboard.

_____

3. The writer published a new novel.

_____

4. **Tulienda dukani.** *(We went to the store.)*

_____

5. **Alishona gauni.** *(She sewed a dress.)*

_____

Chapter 26
PERFECT

The past tense is used to express an action that occurred in the past. The **perfect** (or present perfect) tense is one kind of past tense. It is used to indicate that the action occurred at least once, has just occurred, or began in the past but continues in the present.

Mariamu *has gone* out.

perfect tense of the verb *to go*

IN ENGLISH
The perfect tense is formed by using the word *have* or *has* + the past participle of the verb.

> I *have lived* here for ten years.
> The train *has arrived* at the station.

Sometimes the subject of the verb is contracted with *have* or *has*.

> I have ⇒ I've   the train has ⇒ the train's

KWA KISWAHILI
The perfect tense is called **tensi timilifu**. Its tense marker is -**me**-, which occurs after the subject marker and before the verb. The rule for forming the perfect tense verb is the same for every subject marker, including all the noun classes.

For monosyllabic verbs, use the verbal noun form of the verb.

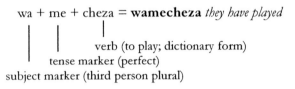

a + me + kuja = **amekuja** *he/she has come*

verb (to come, infinitive)
tense marker (perfect)
subject marker (third person singular)

For verbs with more than one syllable, use the dictionary form of the verb.

wa + me + cheza = **wamecheza** *they have played*

verb (to play; dictionary form)
tense marker (perfect)
subject marker (third person plural)

TAKE NOTE

There are a few Swahili verbs that use the perfect tense with a present tense meaning.

kuchelewa *to be late*   **nimechelewa**
                                    I am late

kukaa *to sit*   **amekaa**
                                    s/he is sitting, s/he sits

kupotea *to be lost*   **mmepotea**
                                    you all are lost

kuchoka *to be tired*   **wamechoka**
                                    they are tired

kuvunjika *to be broken*   **kimevunjika**
                                    it is broken (class 7)

You will need to memorize the verbs that follow this rule.

REVIEW

Read the following paragraph. Circle the verbs that would be in the perfect tense in Swahili.

"We have wandered up and down this street five times. I think that we are lost," I said to my friend. "You've said that already," she answered grouchily. *She has been grumpy all day,* I thought to myself. "Have you ever thought about asking for directions?" I suggested. "We're late, you know," I added. "I know," she answered, "but I have been late before and it didn't matter."

Chapter 27
NEGATIVE PERFECT

Like all verbs, a perfect tense verb can be negated.

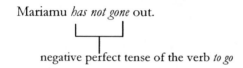

negative perfect tense of the verb *to go*

IN ENGLISH

The perfect tense is made negative by putting *not* or *never* between *has* or *have* and the past participle of the verb.

PERFECT TENSE	NEGATIVE PERFECT TENSE
They *have been* to our new house.	They *have not been* to our new house.
She *has left* the country.	She *has never left* the country.

Sometimes the subject of the verb is contracted with *has* or *have*.

> they have ⇒ they've
> she has ⇒ she's

Sometimes *have* or *has* is contracted with not.

> they have not ⇒ they haven't
> she has not ⇒ she hasn't

KWA KISWAHILI

The negative perfect tense is called **tensi timilifu kanusho**.
Its tense marker is the perfect tense marker -**ja**-, which occurs
after the subject marker but before the verb. It is formed
with the negative prefix **ha**- + the subject marker + the tense
marker -**ja**- + the dictionary form of the verb.

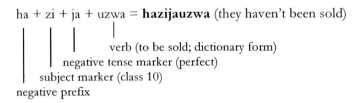

ha + zi + ja + uzwa = **hazijauzwa** (they haven't been sold)

| | | verb (to be sold; dictionary form)
| | negative tense marker (perfect)
| subject marker (class 10)
negative prefix

Verbs with a second person singular subject (you) or a third
person singular subject (he or she) form the past negative in
the same way, but the negative prefix **ha**- combines with the
a- or **u**- sound of the subject markers to create slightly
different results.

ha + u + ja + soma = **hujasoma** *(you haven't studied)*

| | | verb (to study; dictionary form)
| | negative tense marker (perfect)
| subject marker (second person singular)
negative prefix

ha + a + ja + hitimu = **hajahitimu** *(s/he hasn't graduated)*

| | | verb (to graduate; dictionary form)
| | negative tense marker (perfect)
| subject marker (third person singular)
negative prefix

The only subject that forms the past negative differently is the first person singular (I). Instead of adding the negative prefix **ha-**, the first person singular uses the negative subject marker **si-** in place of its positive singular marker **ni-**.

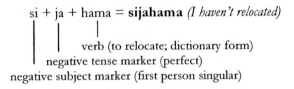

si + ja + hama = **sijahama** *(I haven't relocated)*

verb (to relocate; dictionary form)
negative tense marker (perfect)
negative subject marker (first person singular)

TAKE NOTE

The negative perfect in Swahili often implies that the action has not occurred *yet*, but that it may in the future.

Sijatembelea Tanzania.
I haven't visited Tanzania (yet).
Gari la moshi halijaja.
The train hasn't come (yet).

REVIEW

Rewrite the following sentences putting verbs in the negative perfect tense.

1. I have been to that store many times.

_____

2. We've had a lot of rain this month.

_____

3. A boy has fallen down the well.

_____

4. **Wameenda msikitini.**
    (They have gone to the mosque.)

_____

5. **Baisikeli imepotezwa.**
    (The bicycle has been lost.)

_____

6. **Uhuru umefika.**
    (Freedom has arrived)

_____

Chapter 28
FUTURE

The **future** tense is used to express an action that will occur in the future. For example:

> I *will go* to the store later this afternoon.
> |
> future tense of the verb *to go*

IN ENGLISH
The future tense is formed by using the word *will* + the dictionary form of the verb.

> The party *will start* tomorrow.
> The baby *will crawl* before she walks.

Sometimes the subject of the verb is contracted with *will*.

> *I will* ⟹ *I'll*   *you will* ⟹ *you'll*

KWA KISWAHILI
The future tense is called **wakati ujao.** Its tense marker is -*ta*-. It is formed by combining using the subject marker + the tense marker -*ta*- + the verb. The rule for forming the future tense verb is the same for every subject marker, including all the noun classes.

For monosyllabic verbs, use the verbal noun form of the verb.

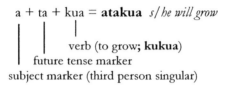

a + ta + kua = **atakua** *s/he will grow*

verb (to grow; **kukua**)
future tense marker
subject marker (third person singular)

For verbs with more than one syllable, use the dictionary form of the verb.

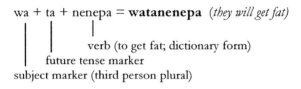

wa + ta + nenepa = **watanenepa** *(they will get fat)*

verb (to get fat; dictionary form)
future tense marker
subject marker (third person plural)

REVIEW

Use the second person singular (you) to create future tense verbs for each of the infinitive verbs listed below.

INFINITIVE   a. ENGLISH FUTURE TENSE
                              b. SWAHILI FUTURE TENSE

to go **kuenda**   a. _____

                             b. _____

to begin **kuanza**   a. _____

                             b. _____

to laugh **kucheka**   a. _____

b. _____

to walk **kutembea**   a. _____

b. _____

to borrow **kukopa**   a. _____

b. _____

Chapter 29
NEGATIVE FUTURE

Like all verb tenses, the future tense can be negated.

She <u>*will not go*</u> to the store later today.
|
negative future tense of the verb *to go*

IN ENGLISH
The future tense is made negative by putting the word *not* between the word *will* and the dictionary form of the verb.

FUTURE TENSE	NEGATIVE FUTURE TENSE
The party *will start* tomorrow	The party *will not start* tomorrow.
The baby *will crawl* after she walks.	The baby *will not crawl* until after she walks.

Sometimes the words *will* and *not* are contracted.

the party will not start ⇒ the party *won't* start
the baby will not crawl ⇒ the baby *won't* crawl

KWA KISWAHILI
The negative future tense is called **wakati ujao kanusho**. It is formed by using the negative prefix *ha-* + the subject marker + the tense marker *-ta-* + the verb.

For monosyllabic verbs, use the verbal noun form of the verb.

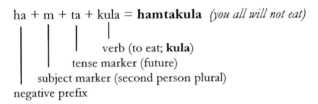

ha + m + ta + kula = **hamtakula** *(you all will not eat)*

verb (to eat; **kula**)
tense marker (future)
subject marker (second person plural)
negative prefix

For verbs with more than one syllable, use the dictionary form of the verb.

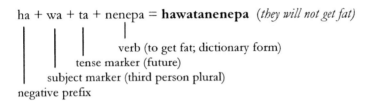

ha + wa + ta + nenepa = **hawatanenepa** *(they will not get fat)*

verb (to get fat; dictionary form)
tense marker (future)
subject marker (third person plural)
negative prefix

Verbs with a second person singular subject (you) or a third person singular subject (he or she) form the past negative in the same way, but the negative prefix *ha*- combines with the *a*- or *u*- sound of the subject markers to create slightly different results.

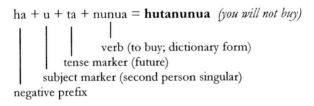

ha + u + ta + nunua = **hutanunua** *(you will not buy)*

verb (to buy; dictionary form)
tense marker (future)
subject marker (second person singular)
negative prefix

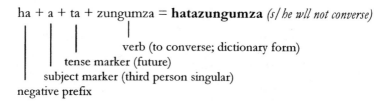

ha + a + ta + zungumza = **hatazungumza** *(s/he will not converse)*

verb (to converse; dictionary form)

tense marker (future)

subject marker (third person singular)

negative prefix

The only subject that forms the past negative differently is the first person singular (I). Instead of adding the negative prefix *ha-*, the first person singular uses the negative subject marker *si-* in place of its positive singular marker *ni-*.

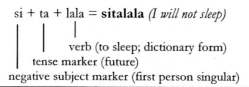

si + ta + lala = **sitalala** *(I will not sleep)*

verb (to sleep; dictionary form)

tense marker (future)

negative subject marker (first person singular)

REVIEW

Rewrite the following sentences using the negative future tense.

1. *Class will begin at 10 a.m.*

2. *The new store will open next week.*

3. *The warm season will be very humid this year.*

4. **Safari itakwisha kesho.**
   (The trip will end tomorrow.)

---

5. **Kitabu kitaanguka chini.**
   (The book will fall down.)

---

6. **Mti utakua pole pole.**
   (The tree will grow slowly.)

Chapter 30
THE VERB 'TO BE'
KUWA

The verb *to be* is an irregular verb, which means that it is conjugated differently than other verbs in some of the tenses. Because it is irregular, it is studied separately from other verbs.

She *is* a good student.

present tense verb *to be*

IN ENGLISH
Like all verbs, the verb *to be* can be conjugated in the present, perfect, past, and future tenses, and in the positive and negative.

Present Tense
The verb *to be* conjugated in the present tense is the English verb which changes the most; it has three forms: *am, are,* and *is.*

I *am*	we *are*
you *are*	you all *are*
he, she, it *is*	they *are*

In conversation the subject and the verb *to be* are often contracted.

I am ⇒ I'm   we are ⇒ we're

you are ⇒ you're

he is ⇒ he's   they are ⇒ they're

she is ⇒ she's

it is ⇒ it's

Negative Present Tense

To negate the present tense of the verb *to be*, simply add the word *not* after the verb *to be*.

I *am not*   we *are not*

you *are not*   you all *are not*

he, she, it *is not*   they *are not*

Present Tense

There are two forms of the verb *to be* in the perfect tense: *have been* and *has been*.

I *have been*   we *have been*

you *have been*   you all *have been*

he/she/it *has been*   they *have been*

In conversation, the subject is sometimes contracted with the helping verbs *have* and *has*.

> *I have been* ⟹ *I've been*
> *you have been* ⟹ *you've been*
> *he has been* ⟹ *he's been*
> *she has been* ⟹ *she's been*
> *it has been* ⟹ *it's been*
> *we have been* ⟹ *we've been*
> *they have been* ⟹ *they've been*

Negative Present Tense

To negate the perfect tense of the verb *to be,* add the word *not* in between *have* or *has* and the verb *to be.*

I *have not been*	we *have not been*
you *have not been*	you all *have not been*
he/she/it *has not been*	they *have not been*

Past Tense

There are two forms of the verb *to be* in the past tense: *was* and *were.*

I *was*	we *were*
you *were*	you all *were*
he/she/it *was*	they *were*

Negative Past Tense

To negate the past tense of the verb *to be*, add the word *not* after the verb *to be*.

I *was not*	we *were not*
you *were not*	you all *were not*
he/she/it *was not*	they *were not*

In conversation the verb *to be* and the word *not* are sometimes contracted.

$$was\ not \Rightarrow wasn't$$
$$were\ not \Rightarrow we\ weren't$$

Future Tense

There is only one form of the verb *to be* in the future tense: *will be*.

I *will be*	we *will be*
you *will be*	you all *will be*
he/she/it *will be*	they *will be*

In conversation sometimes the subject is contracted with *will*.

I will be $\Rightarrow$ *I'll be*	*we will be* $\Rightarrow$ *we'll be*
you will be $\Rightarrow$ *you'll be*	
he will be $\Rightarrow$ *he'll be*	*they will be* $\Rightarrow$ *they'll be*
she will be $\Rightarrow$ *she'll be*	
it will be $\Rightarrow$ *it'll be*	

Negative Future Tense

To negate the future tense of the verb *to be*, add the word *not* in between the word *will* and the verb *to be*.

I *will not be*	we *will not be*
you *will not be*	you all *will not be*
he/she/it *will not be*	they *will not be*

In conversation sometimes the words *will* and *not* are contracted.

will not be ⇒ *won't be*

KWA KISWAHILI

The verb *to be* is **kuwa**; this is the verbal noun form of the word. Like all verbs, the verb *to be* can be conjugated in the present, perfect, past, and future tenses. It is only irregular in the present tense; the other tenses follow the same rules as most verbs.

Present Tense

The verb *to be,* conjugated in the present tense, has only one form for all subjects, including all the noun classes: **ni**.

Mimi *ni* mwanafunzi. *I am a student.*

Wewe *ni* mwanafunzi. *You are a student.*

Yeye *ni* mwanafunzi. *He or she is a student.*

Sisi *ni* wanafunzi. *We are students.*

Ninyi *ni* wanafunzi. *You all are students.*

Wao *ni* wanafunzi. *They are students.*

Kiti *ni* kigumu. *The chair is hard.* (class 7)

Mahali *ni* pazuri. *The place is nice.* (class 16)

Negative Present Tense

To negate the present tense of the verb *to be*, the word *si* is used for all subjects, including all the noun classes.

> **Mimi *si* daktari.** *I am not a doctor.*
> **Wewe *si* daktari.** *You are not a doctor.*
> **Yeye *si* daktari.** *He/she is not a doctor.*
> **Sisi *si* daktari.** *We are not doctors.*
> **Ninyi *si* daktari.** *You all are not doctors.*
> **Wao *si* daktari.** *They are not doctors.*
> **Hii *si* migomba.** *These are not banana trees.* (class 4)

Perfect Tense

To form the perfect tense of the verb *to be*, follow the rules for forming the perfect tense from monosyllabic verbs.

subject marker + *-me-* perfect tense marker + *kuwa*

> **nimekuwa** *I have been*
> **umekuwa** *you have been*
> **wamekuwa** *they have been* (class 2)
> **yamekuwa** *they have been* (class 6)

Negative Perfect Tense

There are two possible ways to negate the perfect tense of the verb *to be*. One way is to follow the rules for negating the perfect tense of monosyllabic verbs.

negative prefix *ha-* + subject marker + *-ja-* tense marker + *wa*

hatujawa *we haven't been*
hamjawa *you all haven't been*
hawajawa *they haven't been* (class 2)
hazijawa *they haven't been* (class 10)

Or you can keep the **ku**- prefix of the verbal noun form of the verb **kuwa**.

negative prefix *ha-* + subject marker + *-ja-* tense marker + *kuwa*

hatujakuwa *we haven't been*
hamjakuwa *you all haven't been*
hawajakuwa *they haven't been* (class 2)
hazijakuwa *they haven't been* (class 10)

Remember that the formation of the first person (I), second person (you) and third person (he or she) is slightly different.

sijawa or **sijakuwa** *I haven't been*
hujawa or **hujakuwa** *you haven't been*
hajawa or **hajakuwa** *he/she hasn't been*

Past Tense

To form the past tense of the verb *to be*, follow the rules for forming the past tense from monosyllabic verbs.

subject marker + *-li-* tense marker + *kuwa*

> **alikuwa** *he was*
> **tulikuwa** *we were*
> **mlikuwa** *you all were*
> **ilikuwa** *they were* (class 4) or *it was* (class 9)

Negative Past Tense

To negate the past tense of the verb *to be*, follow the rules for forming the negative past tense from monosyllabic verbs.

negative prefix *ha-* + subject marker + *-ku-* tense marker + *wa*

> **hatukuwa** *we weren't*
> **hamkuwa** *you all weren't*
> **hawakuwa** *they weren't* (class 2)
> **halikuwa** *it wasn't* (class 5)

Remember that the formation of the first person (I), second person (you) and third person (he or she) are slightly different.

> **sikuwa** *I wasn't*
> **hukuwa** *you weren't*
> **hakuwa** *he or she wasn't*

Future Tense

To form the future tense of the verb *to be*, follow the rules for forming the future tense from monosyllabic verbs.

subject marker + *-ta-* tense marker + *kuwa*

> **watakuwa** *they will be* (class 2)
> **utakuwa** *it will be* (class 11 or 14)
> **zitakuwa** *they will be* (class 10)
> **kutakuwa** *it will be* (class 15)

Negative Future Tense

To negate the future tense of the verb *to be*, follow the rules for forming the negative future tense from monosyllabic verbs.

negative prefix *ha-* + subject marker + *-ta-* tense marker + ku*wa*

> **hamtakuwa** *you all will not be*
> **hawatakuwa** *they will not be* (class 2)
> **hazitakuwa** *they will not be* (class 10)
> **hakutakuwa** *it will not be* (class 15)

Remember that the formation of the first person (I), second person (you) and third person (he or she) are slightly different.

> **sitakuwa** *I will not be*
> **hutakuwa** *you will not be*
> **hatakuwa** *he or she will not be*

REVIEW

Fill in the blanks to conjugate the verb *to be* in both English and Swahili.

a. *I* _____ *a teacher.*

b. **Mimi** _____ **mwalimu.**

1. present tense   a. _____

                        b. _____

2. negative present   a. _____

                        b. _____

3. perfect tense   a. _____

                        b. _____

4. negative perfect   a. _____

                        b. _____

5. past tense   a. _____

                        b. _____

6. negative past   a. _____

                        b. _____

7. future tense   a. _____

                                        b. _____

8. negative future   a. _____

                                        b. _____

Chapter 31
THE LOCATIVE VERB 'TO BE'

One use of the verb *to be* is to state a noun's location. For example:

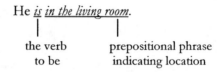

He *is* *in the living room*.

   the verb   prepositional phrase
   to be   indicating location

IN ENGLISH

In order to express a noun's location, use the verb *to be* with a preposition or a prepositional phrase. These prepositions include *at, in, on, above, below, near, under, behind, among, between, beside*, etc.. The prepositional phrases include *next to, in front of, to the side*, etc. Regardless of the preposition used, the verb *to be* is conjugated normally. (See Chapter 30, The Verb 'to be'.)

I am in the house.   *I am not in the house*
I have been among the trees. *I have not been among the trees.*
I was on the roof.   *I was not on the roof.*
I will be under the awning. *I will not be under the awning.*

KWA KISWAHILI

In order to express a noun's location, a locative suffix is added to the verb *to be*, **kuwa**. There are three locative suffixes: **-po**, **-ko** and **-mo**. These form three locative verbs: **kuwapo**, **kuwako**, and **kuwamo**.

The suffix **-po** is used to refer to either a specific location or one that is close to the speaker. It is used even if the verb is followed by a word that means *here*.

> **Majengo ya*po* hapa.**
> *The buildings are here.*
> **Nitakuwa*po* Dar es Salaam.**
> *I will be (here) in Dar es Salaam.*

The suffix **-ko** is used to refer to either a general location or one that is far from the speaker.

> **Alikuwa*ko* maktabani.** *He was at the library.*
> **Miti i*ko* msituni.** *The trees are in the forest.*

The suffix **-mo** is used to refer to emphasize that the noun is inside or on the surface of a location.

> **Kitabu ki*mo* mfukoni.**
> *The book is in the bag.*
> **Glasi ilikuwa*mo* mezani.**
> *The glass was on the table.*

As you can see, the **-po**, **-ko**, and **-mo** suffixes can be used to translate the English prepositions *in, at,* or *on.* Other prepositions and prepositional phrases will be translated using Swahili prepositions in combination with the locative verbs.

Alikuwa*ko baina* **yetu.** *She was between us.*

| |
locative verb suffix   preposition (**baina**, *between*)

Present Tense

To form the present tense of the locative verb, combine the subject marker + the locative suffix. The only subject marker that is different from the ones you have already learned is the third person singular (he or she; class 1) which is **yu-** instead of **a-**.

KUWAPO	KUWAKO	KUWAMO
nipo *I am here*		**nimo** *I am inside*
upo *you are here*	**uko** *you are there*	**umo** *you are inside*
yupo *s/he is here*	**yuko** *s/he is there*	**yumo** *s/he is inside*
tupo *we are here*		**tumo** *we are inside*
mpo *you all are here*	**mko** *you all are there*	**mmo** *you all are inside*
wapo *they are here*	**wako** *they are there*	**wamo** *they are inside*
lipo *it is here* (class 5)	**liko** *it is there* (class 5)	**limo** *it is inside* (class 5)

Negative Present Tense

To negate the present tense of the locative verb, add the negative prefix **ha-**. Remember that the first person singular (I), second person singular (you), and third person singular (he or she) have slightly different negative prefixes.

KUWAPO	KUWAKO	KUWAMO
sipo *I am not here*		**simo** *I am not inside*
hupo *you are not here*	**huko** *you are not there*	**humo** *you are not inside*
hayupo *he/she is not here*	**hayuko** *he/she is not there*	**hayumo** *he/she is not inside*
hatupo *we are not here*		**hatumo** *we are not inside*
hampo *you all are not here*	**hamko** *you all are not there*	**hammo** *you all are not inside*
hawapo *they are not here*	**hawako** *they are not there*	**hawamo** *they are not inside*
halipo *it is not here* (class 5)	**haliko** *it is not there* (class 5)	**halimo** *it is not inside* (class 5)

Other Tenses

Only in the present tense and negative present tense is the locative verb conjugated differently from the regular verb **kuwa**. All other tenses are conjugated in the same way as they are for the verb **kuwa**, but –**po, -ko,** or -**mo** are added as suffixes.

PERFECT   **wamekuwapo**
                     they have been here
NEGATIVE PERFECT   **hawajawapo**
                     they have not been here
PAST   **walikuwako**
                     they were there
NEGATIVE PAST   **hawakuwako**
                     they were not there

FUTURE	**watakuwamo**
	they will be inside
NEGATIVE FUTURE	**hawatakuwamo**
	they will not be inside

REVIEW

Circle the locative suffix you would use if translating these sentences into Swahili.

1. *The boys are at the pool.*	-po	-ko	-mo
2. *I am at home.*	-po	-ko	-mo
3. *Where are you?*	-po	-ko	-mo
4. *We are in Kenya.*	-po	-ko	-mo
5. *Mt. Kilimanjaro is in Tanzania.*	-po	-ko	-mo
6. *The oranges are in the sack.*	-po	-ko	-mo
7. *What is biting you is in your clothes.*[12]	-po	-ko	-mo
8. *We are in the store.*	-po	-ko	-mo
9. *The university is right here.*	-po	-ko	-mo
10. *The library is right over there.*	-po	-ko	-mo

---

[12] An English translation of a Swahili proverb.

Chapter 32
THE VERB 'TO HAVE'

The verb *to have* is used to indicate that one noun possesses another noun. It is an **irregular verb**, which means that it is conjugated differently than other verbs in some tenses. Because it is irregular, it is studied separately from other verbs.

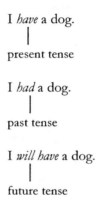

I *have* a dog.

present tense

I *had* a dog.

past tense

I *will have* a dog.

future tense

IN ENGLISH
Like all verbs, the verb *to have* can be conjugated in the present, perfect, past, and future tenses, and in the positive and negative.

Present Tense
The verb *to have*, conjugated in the present tense, has two forms: *have* and *has*.

I *have*	we *have*
you *have*	you all *have*
he, she, it *has*	they *have*

Negative Present Tense

To negate the present tense of the verb *to have*, add the words *do not* before the verb *have*.

I *do not have*   we *do not have*
you *do not have*   you all *do not have*
he, she, it *does not have*   they *do not have*

In conversation sometimes the words *do* or *does* are contracted with the word *not*.

> *do not have* ⟹ *don't have*
> *does not have* ⟹ *doesn't have*

Perfect Tense

There are two forms of the verb *to have* in the perfect tense: *have had* and *has had*.

I *have had*   we *have had*
you *have had*   you all *have had*
he/she/it *has had*   they *have had*

In conversation sometimes the subject is contracted with the helping verbs *have* and *has*.

> *I have had* ⟹ *I've had*
> *you have had* ⟹ *you've had*
> *he has had* ⟹ *he's had*
> *she has had* ⟹ *she's had*
> *it has had* ⟹ *it's had*
> *we have had* ⟹ *we've had*
> *they have had* ⟹ *they've had*

Negative Perfect Tense

To negate the perfect tense of the verb *to have*, add the word *not* in between *have* or *has* and the verb *had*.

I *have not had*	we *have not had*
you *have not had*	you all *have not had*
he/she/it *has not had*	they *have not had*

In conversation sometimes the words *have* or *has* are contracted with *not*.

have not had ⇒ *haven't had*
has not had ⇒ *hasn't had*

Past Tense

There is only one form of the verb *to have* in the past tense: *had*.

I *had*	we *had*
you *had*	you all *had*
he/she/it *had*	they *had*

Negative Past Tense

To negate the past tense of the verb *to have*, add the words *did not* before the verb *have*.

I *did not have*	we *did not have*
you *did not have*	you all *did not have*
he/she/it *did not have*	they *did not have*

In conversation the words *did* and *not* are sometimes contracted.

did not have ⇒ didn't have

Future Tense

There is only one form of the verb *to have* in the future tense: *will have*.

I *will have*	we *will have*
you *will have*	you all *will have*
he/she/it *will have*	they *will have*

In conversation sometimes the subject is contracted with *will*.

I will have ⇒ I'll have
you will have ⇒ you'll have
he will have ⇒ he'll have
she will have ⇒ she'll have
it will have ⇒ it'll have
we will have ⇒ we'll have
they will have ⇒ they'll have

Negative Future Tense

To negate the future tense of the verb *to have*, add the word *not* in between the word *will* and the verb *have*.

I *will not have*   we *will not have*
you *will not have*   you all *will not have*
he/she/it *will not have*   they *will not have*

In conversation sometimes the words *will* and *not* are contracted to form the word *won't.*

> *I will not have* ⟹ *I won't have*
> *you will not have* ⟹ *you won't have*
> *he/she/it will not have* ⟹ *he/she/it won't have*
> *we will not have* ⟹ *we won't have*
> *they will not have* ⟹ *they won't have*

KWA KISWAHILI

The verb *to have* is used to indicate that one noun possesses another noun. It is an irregular verb, which means that it is conjugated differently than other verbs in some tenses. Because it is irregular, it is studied separately from other verbs.

The infinitive of the verb *to have* in Swahili is **kuwa na**, which literally means *to be with*. It is considered an irregular verb because, only most verbs, in the present tense the conjugated verb is not formed from this infinitive. Instead, in the present tense the verb acts as if its infinitive is **kuna**.

Like all verbs, the verb to have can be conjugated in the present, perfect, past, and future tenses, and in the positive and negative.

Present Tense

The verb **kuwa na**, conjugated in the present tense, is formed by combining the subject prefix with the stem –**na**. Subject prefixes are explained in Chapter 20.

nina	I have	**tuna**	we have
una	you have	**mna**	you all have
ana	he or she has	**wana**	they have
ina	it has (class 9)	**zina**	they have (class 10)

Negative Present Tense

To negate the present tense of the verb **kuwa na**, combine the negative marker *ha–* with the subject prefix and the stem –*na*.

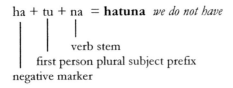

```
ha + tu + na  = hatuna  we do not have
 |    |    |
 |    |    verb stem
 |    first person plural subject prefix
 negative marker
```

The formation of the first person (I), second person (you) and third person (he or she) is slightly different, just as it is for regular verbs.

sina *I don't have*
huna *you don't have*
hana *he or she doesn't have*

Perfect Tense

To form the perfect tense of the verb *to have*, follow the rules for forming the perfect tense from monosyllabic verbs.

subject marker + *-me-* perfect tense marker + *kuwa na*

nimekuwa na *I have had*
umekuwa na *you have had*
wamekuwa na *they have had* (class 2)
yamekuwa na *they have had* (class 6)

Negative Perfect Tense

There are two possible ways to negate the perfect tense of the verb *to have*. One way is to follow the rules for negating the perfect tense of monosyllabic verbs.

negative prefix *ha-* + subject marker + *-ja-* tense marker + *wa na*

hatujawa na *we haven't had*
hamjawa na *you all haven't had*
hawajawa na *they haven't had* (class 2)
hazijawa na *they haven't had* (class 10)

Or you can keep the **ku-** prefix of the verbal noun form of
the verb **kuwa na**.

negative prefix *ha-* + subject marker + *-ja-* tense marker +
kuwa na

hatujakuwa na *we haven't had*
hamjakuwa na *you all haven't had*
hawajakuwa na *they haven't had* (class 2)
hazijakuwa na *they haven't had* (class 10)

Remember that the formation of the first person (I), second
person (you) and third person (he or she) is slightly different.

sijawa na or **sijakuwa na** *I haven't had*
hujawa na or **hujakuwa na** *you haven't had*
hajawa na or **hajakuwa na** *he/she hasn't had*

Past Tense
To form the past tense of the verb *to have*, follow the rules for
forming the past tense from monosyllabic verbs.

subject marker + *-li-* tense marker + *kuwa na*

alikuwa na *he had*
tulikuwa na *we had*
mlikuwa na *you all had*
ilikuwa na *they had* (class 4) or *it had* (class 9)

Negative Past Tense

To negate the past tense of the verb *to be*, follow the rules for forming the negative past tense from monosyllabic verbs.

> negative prefix *ha-* + subject marker + *-ku-* tense marker + *wa na*

> > **hatukuwa na** *we did not have*
> > **hamkuwa na** *you all did not have*
> > **hawakuwa na** *they did not have* (class 2)
> > **halitakuwa na** *it didn't have* (class 5)

Remember that the formation of the first person (I), second person (you) and third person (he or she) are slightly different.

> > **sikuwa na** *I didn't have*
> > **hukuwa na** *you didn't have*
> > **hakuwa na** *he or didn't have*

Future Tense

To form the future tense of the verb *to be*, follow the rules for forming the future tense from monosyllabic verbs.

> subject marker + *-ta-* tense marker + *kuwa na*

> > **watakuwa na** *they will have* (class 2)
> > **utakuwa na** *it will have* (class 11 or 14)
> > **zitakuwa na** *they will have* (class 10)
> > **kutakuwa na** *it will have* (class 15)

Negative Future Tense

To negate the future tense of the verb *to have*, follow the rules for forming the negative future tense from monosyllabic verbs.

negative prefix *ha-* + subject marker + *-ta-* tense marker + *kuwa na*

hamtakuwa na *you all will not have*
hawatakuwa na *they will not have* (class 2)
hazitakuwa na *they will not have* (class 10)
hakutakuwa na *it will not have* (class 15)

Remember that the formation of the first person (I), second person (you) and third person (he or she) are slightly different.

sitakuwa na *I will not have*
hutakuwa na *you will not have*
hatakuwa na *he or she will not have*

REVIEW

Fill in the blanks to conjugate the verb *to have* in both English and Swahili.

a. *You* _____ *a book.*

b. **Wewe** _____ **kitabu.**

1. present tense   a. _____

                           b. _____

2. negative present   a. _____

b. _____

3. perfect tense   a. _____

                                  b. _____

4. negative perfect   a. _____

                                  b. _____

5. past tense   a. _____

                                  b. _____

6. negative past   a. _____

                                  b. _____

7. future tense   a. _____

                                  b. _____

8. negative future   a. _____

                                  b. _____

Chapter 33
AUXILIARY VERBS

A verb is called an **auxiliary verb** or **helping verb** when it helps another verb form one of its tenses. (See Chapter 21, *Introduction to Verbs and Verb Tenses,* and Chapter 43, *Compound Tenses.*) When it is used alone, it functions as a main verb.

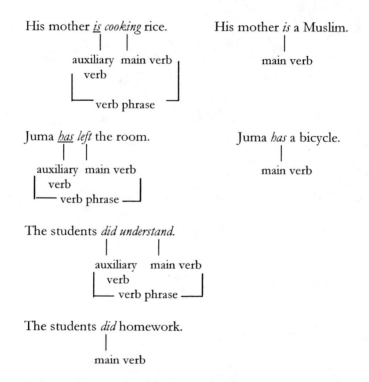

An auxiliary verb plus a main verb form a **compound verb**, also called a **verb phrase**.

IN ENGLISH

There are several auxiliary verbs: forms of *to have, to be,* and *to do,* as well as a series of auxiliary words such as *will, would, may, might, must, can,* and *could,* which are used to change the meaning of the main verb.

Auxiliary verbs and words serve seven purposes:

1. to indicate the tense of the main verb in a verb phrase. See Chapter 21, *Introduction to Verb and Verb Tenses.*

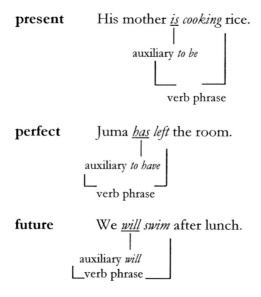

   present   His mother *is cooking* rice.

                      auxiliary *to be*

                      verb phrase

   perfect   Juma *has left* the room.

                      auxiliary *to have*

                      verb phrase

   future   We *will swim* after lunch.

                      auxiliary *will*

                      verb phrase

2. to help form the perfect tenses. See Chapter 43, *Compound Tenses*.

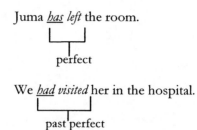

Juma *has left* the room.

perfect

We *had visited* her in the hospital.

past perfect

3. to help form the progressive forms of the present, past, and future tenses. See Chapter 22, *Present,* and Chapter 43, *Compound Tenses.*

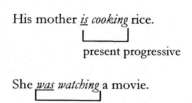

His mother *is cooking* rice.

present progressive

She *was watching* a movie.

past progressive

They *will be travelling.*

future progressive

4. to indicate the passive voice. See Chapter 44.

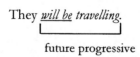

Sudi *is liked* by his classmates.

present passive

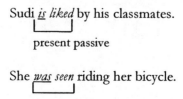

She *was seen* riding her bicycle.

past passive

5. to help form questions and to make sentences negative. See Chapters 49 and 50.

> <u>Does</u> Zakia *like* breadfruit?
> Zakia <u>*does not*</u> *like* breadfruit.

6. to help form the emphatic forms of the present and past tenses. See Chapter 22, *Present,* and Chapter 24, *Past Tense.*

> His mother <u>*does*</u> *like* to cook rice.

> present emphatic

> Juma <u>*did*</u> *leave* the room.

> past emphatic

5. to help form ideas of possibility or probability. See Chapter 39, *The Subjunctive Mood.*

> Our friends <u>*may*</u> *visit* next week.

KWA KISWAHILI
Most tenses or ideas that are composed of a verb phrase in English are expressed by a single verb in Swahili.

> His mother <u>*is*</u> *cooking* rice.
> - in English: present progressive
> - in Swahili: present → **anapika** or **apika**

Juma *has left* the room.
- in English: perfect
- in Swahili: perfect → **ameondoka**

We *will swim* after lunch.
- in English: future
- in Swahili: future → **tutaogolea**

Sudi *is liked* by his classmates.
- in English: present passive
- in Swahili: present passive → **anapendwa**

She *was seen* riding her bicycle.
- in English: past passive
- in Swahili: past passive → **alionwa**

Does Zakia *like* breadfruit?
- in English: present interrogative
- in Swahili: present → **anapenda**

Zakia *does not like* breadfruit.
- in English: present negative
- in Swahili: present negative → **hapendi**

His mother *does like* to cook rice.
- in English: present emphatic
- in Swahili: present → **anapenda** or **apenda**

Our friends *may visit* next week.
- in English: subjunctive
- in Swahili: present conditional → **wangetembelea**

Perfect and progressive forms, however, are expressed with a **verb phrase** or **compound tense**, which are explained in Chapter 43. In verb phrases, the verb **kuwa** (to be) functions as an auxiliary verb.

<u>Tulikuwa</u> tukienda shuleni.
We were going to school.

REVIEW

Underline the verbs and verb phrases in the following paragraph. Circle the auxiliary verbs.

Because Chausika was always asking his wife to go to the shop, his brother Mashaka had thought about buying him a bicycle. Mashaka went to the local bicycle repair shop and tried to buy a used bicycle. After bargaining he was finally able to get the bike for a good price. "My brother will ride this bike every day," he thought to himself. Now Chausika does not need to ask his wife to go to the shop.

Chapter 34
OBJECTS

The **object** of a sentence is the person, idea or object toward whom or which the action of the verb is directed. It answers the question *whom?* or *what?* asked after a verb or preposition.

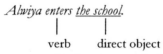

Alwiya enters the school.

          verb   direct object

- Alwiya enters *what?* The school.
- *The school* is the direct object of the verb *enters.*

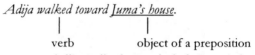

Adija walked toward Juma's house.

        verb   object of a preposition

- Adija walked *toward what?* Juma's house.
- *Juma's house* is the object of the preposition *toward.*

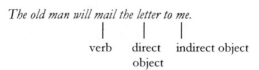

The old man will mail the letter to me.

        verb   direct   indirect object
                 object

- The old man will mail *what?* The letter.
- *The letter* is the direct object of the verb *will mail.*
- The old man will mail the letter *to whom?* Me.
- *Me* is the indirect object of the verb *will mail.*

The three types of objects will be studied separately: **direct object** (Chapter 35), **indirect object** (Chapter 36), and **object of the preposition** (Chapter 48).

IN ENGLISH
An **object** is a noun or a pronoun.

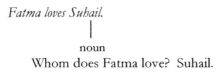

Fatma loves Suhail.

noun
Whom does Fatma love? Suhail.

Fatma loves him.

pronoun
Whom does Fatma love? Him.

KWA KISWAHILI
An object is called **mtenda** or **shamirisho**. The plural, *objects,* are **watenda** or **shamirisho.**

An object can be a noun or pronoun, but it can also be represented by an object marker that agrees with the noun or pronoun in class.

Fatma anampenda Suhail. *Fatma loves Suhail.*
Fatma anampenda yeye. *Fatma loves him.*
Fatma anampenda. *Fatma loves him.*

Every personal pronoun and every noun class has an object marker that can be used to express a direct object. An object marker is called **kiambishi kati cha shamirisho**; the plural is **viambishi kati vya shamirisho.**

OBJECT	OBJECT MARKER	VERB WITH OBJECT MARKER
me	-ni-	ana<u>ni</u>penda *s/he loves me*
you	-ku-	ana<u>ku</u>penda *s/he loves you*
him/her (class 1)	-m- or -mw-	ana<u>m</u>penda *s/he loves him/her*
us	-tu-	ana<u>tu</u>penda *s/he loves us*
you all	-wa- *or* -ku	ana<u>wa</u>pendeni *s/he loves you all*
them (class 2)	-wa-	ana<u>wa</u>penda *s/he loves them*
it (class 3)	-u-	ana<u>u</u>penda *s/he loves it*
them (class 4)	-i-	ana<u>i</u>penda *s/he loves it*
it (class 5)	-li-	ana<u>li</u>penda *s/he loves it*
them (class 6)	-ya-	ana<u>ya</u>penda *s/he loves it*
it (class 7)	-ki-	ana<u>ki</u>penda *s/he loves it*
them (class 8)	-vi-	ana<u>vi</u>penda *s/he loves it*
it (class 9)	-i-	ana<u>i</u>penda *s/he loves it*
them (class 10)	-zi-	ana<u>zi</u>penda *s/he loves it*
it (class 11)	-u-	ana<u>u</u>penda *s/he loves it*
it (class 14)	-u-	ana<u>u</u>penda *s/he loves it*

it (class 15)	**-ku-**	**ana<u>ku</u>penda**
		s/he loves it
it (class 16)	**-pa-**	**ana<u>pa</u>penda**
		s/he loves it
it (class 17)	**-ku-**	**ana<u>ku</u>penda**
		s/he loves it
it (class 18)	**-mu-**	**ana<u>mu</u>penda**
		s/he loves it

The object marker goes between the tense marker and the dictionary form of the verb, following this structure:

> subject marker + tense marker + object marker + dictionary formof the verb

Object markers can be used with any tense, in the affirmative or negative.

present	**na<u>mw</u>ona or nina<u>mw</u>ona**
	I see him
present negative	**si<u>mw</u>oni**
	I don't see him
perfect	**nime<u>mw</u>ona**
	I have seen him
perfect negative	**sija<u>mw</u>ona**
	I haven't seen him
past	**nili<u>mw</u>ona**
	I saw him
past negative	**siku<u>mw</u>ona**
	I didn't see him
future	**nita<u>mw</u>ona**
	I will see him
future negative	**sita<u>mw</u>ona**
	I will not see him

There are three situations in which object markers are used.

1. An object marker <u>must</u> be used when the direct object is a person or a personal pronoun.

    Tunamfahamu Adija. *We know Adija.*
    Tunamfahamu yeye. *We know her.*
    Tunamfahamu. *We know her.*

2. If the direct object is understood, an object marker can be used in place of the noun that is the direct object; in this case it functions like a pronoun in English.

    instead of: **Walinunua vitabu.** *They bought books.*
    you can say: **Walivinunua.** *They bought them.*

3. An object marker can be used together with a direct object for emphasis.

    Alizitaka ndizi. *He wanted <u>bananas</u>* (as opposed to apples).

REVIEW

Underline the objects in the sentences below.

1. I took Zakia to the party in town.

2. Abunawas bought a donkey at the market.

3. The rooster crowed at dawn, waking the whole family.

4. Bring your books to class tomorrow.

5. The teacher invited us to her house for a party.

Chapter 35
DIRECT OBJECTS

A **direct object** is an object that receives the action of the verb directly. It answers the question *whom?* or *what?* asked after the verb.

> *Musa is reading the book.*
> - Musa is reading what? The book.
> - *The book* is the direct object.

> *Mariamu likes Usi.*
> - Mariamu likes whom? Usi.
> - *Usi* is the direct object.

Verbs can be classified according to whether or not they take a direct object.

A **transitive verb** is a verb that takes a direct object. It is indicated by the abbreviation *v.t.* (verb transitive) in dictionaries. You learned about transitive verbs in Chapter 21 (Introduction to Verbs and Verb Tenses).

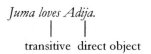
Juma loves Adija.
transitive direct object

An **intransitive verb** is a verb that does not take a direct object. It is indicated by the abbreviation *v.i.* (verb intransitive) in dictionaries. You learned about intransitive verbs in Chapter 21 (Introduction to Verbs and Verb Tenses).

Juma fell.
|
intransitive

IN ENGLISH

A **direct object** is a noun or pronoun that receives the action of the verb without a preposition between the verb and the noun or pronoun object.

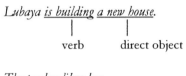

Lubaya is building a new house.
| |
verb   direct object

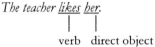

The teacher likes her.
| |
verb   direct object

KWA KISWAHILI

A direct object is called **shamirisho yambwa.** As in English, a direct object is a noun or pronoun that receives the action of the verb directly, without a preposition. (Prepositions are explained in Chapter 47.) It answers the question **nani?** *(who?)* or **nini?** *(what?)* asked after the verb.

Nilikopa pesa. *I borrowed money.*
- **Nilikopa nini? Pesa.**
- No preposition separates **pesa** from the verb **kukopa.**
- Therefore, **pesa** is the direct object.

Abdul atanunua machungwa. *Abdul will buy oranges.*
- **Atanunua nini? Machungwa.**
- No preposition separates **machungwa** from the verb **kununua.**
- Therefore, **machungwa** is the direct object.

As with English verbs, Swahili verbs can be transitive or intransitive depending on whether or not they are followed by a direct object.

The object marker, covered in Chapter 34, is used only for direct objects.

TAKE NOTE

English and Swahili do not have the same relationship between a verb and its object. For example, a verb may take an indirect object in English but a direct object in Swahili, or an object of a preposition in English but a direct object in Swahili. Therefore, when you learn a Swahili verb it is important to find out if its meaning incorporates a preposition. Your textbook and dictionaries will indicate when the meaning of a Swahili verb incorporates a preposition.

Here are some differences you are likely to encounter.

1. ENGLISH: object of a preposition ⇒
    SWAHILI: direct object

    He is looking *for coffee.*
    - Function in English: object of a preposition
    - *He is looking for what? Coffee.*
    - *Coffee* is the object of the preposition *for.*

    Anatafuta kahawa.
    - Function in Swahili: direct object
    - **Anatafuta nini? Kahawa.**
    - The verb **kutafuta** is not followed by a preposition; therefore, its object is a direct object.

    Many common verbs require an object of a preposition in English, but a direct object in Swahili.

to look at	**kuangalia**
to wait for	**kusubiri**

2. ENGLISH: indirect object ⇒SWAHILI: direct object

    We gave *him* five hundred shillings.
    - Function in English: indirect object
    - *We gave books to whom? Him*
    - *Him* is the indirect object of the verb *to give (five hundred shillings* is the direct object).

Tuli*m*pa shilingi mia tano.

- Function in Swahili: direct object.
- **Tulimpa nani shilingi mia tano? Yeye** (expressed with the class 1 object marker *–m*).
- The verb **kupa** is not followed by a preposition; therefore; its object is a direct object.

Several common verbs require an indirect object in English but a direct object in Swahili.

to listen to	**kusikiliza**
to give to	**kupa**

REVIEW

Underline the direct object in each of the following sentences.

1. She gave me a present.

2. Zulekha is reading the newspaper.

3. Pili will drive the car.

4. Hud visited his grandmother.

5. Ammar wrote a letter to his sister.

Chapter 36
INDIRECT OBJECTS

An **indirect object** is a noun or pronoun that receives the action of the verb indirectly.

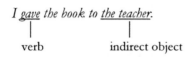

IN ENGLISH
An **indirect object** is a noun or pronoun that receives the action of the verb with the preposition *to* relating it to the verb. It answers the question *to whom?* or *to what?* asked after the verb.

She talked *to the teacher* after school.
- She talked to whom? The teacher.
- *The teacher* is the indirect object.

He returned books *to the library*.
- He returned books to what? The library.
- *The library* is the indirect object.

KWA KISWAHILI
An indirect object is called **shamirisho yambiwa.** It is used as a second object after a direct object. It does not follow prepositions, because the meaning of the preposition *to* or *for* is included in the verb itself. It answers the question *what?* asked after the direct object.

Some verbs are naturally prepositional, like **kupa**, which means *to give*.

> **Uilimpa daktari pesa zangu.**
> *You gave the doctor my money.*
> - **Ulimpa daktari nini? Pesa zangu.**

Other verbs are made prepositional with an **applied extension**, also known as a **prepositional extension** or **mnyambuliko wa kufanyia.**

> **Babangu alininulia baisikeli.**
> *My father bought me a bicycle.*
> - **Babangu alininulia nini? Baisikeli.**
> - **kununulia** = to buy for (from **kununua**, to buy)

Prepositional verbs are explained in Chapter 41 (Verb Extensions).

REVIEW

Underline the indirect object in each of the following sentences.

1. Lioba read a story to her grandmother in the hospital.

2. I sent a letter to my family last week.

3. The teacher gave me a good grade in the course.

4. The children will speak to you about borrowing your toy.

5. Juma drove the car to the store.

Chapter 37
INTRODUCTION TO MOOD

In the grammatical sense, **mood** is a term applied to verb tenses. Different moods serve different purposes. For instance, the verb tenses which state a fact belong to one mood, and the verb tense which gives orders belongs to another. Some moods have multiple tenses, while others have only one tense. For example:

> *You are studying.* (indicative mood)
> *Study!* (imperative mood)
> *I wish you would study.* (subjunctive mood)

You should recognize the names of moods so that you will know what your Swahili textbook is referring to when it uses these terms. You will learn when to use the various moods as you learn verbs and their tenses.

IN ENGLISH
Verbs can be in one of three moods.

1. The **indicative mood** is used to state the factual action of the verb. This is the most common mood, and most of the verb forms that you use in everyday conversation belong to the indicative mood. The majority of the tenses studied in this book belong to the indicative mood: for instance, the present tense (Chapter 22), the perfect tense (Chapter 26), the past tense (Chapter 24), and the future tense (Chapter 28).

Zuhura is *travelling* to Uganda.

present indicative

Abdul-Swammad *has gone* out.

perfect indicative

The workman *finished* his job.

past indicative

You *will arrive* tomorrow.

future indicative

2. The **imperative mood** is used to give commands or orders. It is explained in Chapter 38. This mood is not divided into tenses.

    Sudi, *wash* the dishes!

3. The **subjunctive mood** is used to express a wish, hope, uncertainty or other similar attitude toward a fact or idea. It is explained in Chapter 39. This mood is not divided into tenses.

    I want you *to go* to the store.
    The doctor suggested that my father *not eat salt*.

KWA KISWAHILI
Verbs can be in one of four moods, called **hali**.

1. As in English, the **indicative mood** is the most common. The majority of the tenses studied in this book belong to the indicative mood: for instance, the present tense (Chapter 22), the perfect tense (Chapter 26), the past tense (Chapter 24), and the future tense (Chapter 28). In Swahili the indicative mood is called **hali ya kuarifu.**

2. As in English, the **imperative mood** is used to give orders and it is not divided into tenses (see Chapter 38). In Swahili it is called **hali ya amri.**

3. As in English, the **subjunctive mood** is used to express a wish, hope, uncertainty or other similar attitude toward a fact or idea. Unlike English, it can also be used to give orders. It is not divided into tenses (see Chapter 39). In Swahili it is called **hali ya dhamira tegemezi.**

4. Swahili grammar also has a mood called the **conditional mood**, which has two tenses: the present conditional and the past conditional (see Chapter 40). In Swahili it is called **hali ya sharti.**

▶ When there is no references to mood, the tense belongs to the most common mood, the indicative.

Chapter 38
IMPERATIVE MOOD

The imperative is the mood of the verb used for commands or orders. For example:

Come here!

imperative mood of the verb *to come*

IN ENGLISH
There are two types of commands. The type of command used depends on who is being told to do, or not to do, something.

1. When an order is given to people other than the speaker, the dictionary form of the verb is used.

    Zawadi, *close* your book!
    Students, *study* hard for tomorrow's exam!

In these sentences neither *Zawadi* nor *students* is the subject; the speaker is merely calling out their names. Rather the subject is *you*, which is understood.

To negate this kind of imperative, add the word *don't* before the dictionary form of the verb.

    Zawadi, *don't close* your book!
    Students, *don't study* hard for tomorrow's exam!

4. When an order is given to oneself as well as to others, the phrase *let's* (a contraction of *let us*) precedes the dictionary form of the verb.

>   *Let's go* to the movies.

To negate this kind of imperative, add the word *not* between the phrase *let's* and the verb.

>   *Let's not go* to the movies.

KWA KISWAHILI

The imperative mood is called **hali ya amri**. The same two forms of commands exist. However, only commands given to people other than the speaker are expressed by the imperative mood. The *let's* command is expressed by the subjunctive, which is discussed in Chapter 39.

The command to a another person or other people uses the **imperative mood**, separated into singular and plural. The imperative singular of most verbs is the dictionary form.

>   **Kimbia!** *Run!* **Simama!** *Stand up!*

The imperative plural is usually the dictionary form minus the final *-a* + *-eni*.

>   **Kimbieni!** *Run!*   **Simameni!** *Stand up!*

To form the imperative plurals of verbs that do not end in *-a*, simply add *-ni*.

> **Karibuni!** *Welcome!* (Literally, *come near!*)
> **Jibuni!** *Answer!*

However, some verbs are irregular; you will need to memorize their imperative forms.

> **Nenda! Nendeni!** (from **kuenda**, to go)
> **Njoo! Njooni!** (from **kuja**, to come)

Your textbook and teacher will introduce you to other irregular imperatives.

TAKE NOTE

Negative commands and commands that take object markers are expressed in the subjunctive mood rather than in the imperative mood. You will learn about the subjunctive mood in Chapter 39.

REVIEW

Change the sentences below to the imperative mood.

1. The children are playing dominoes.

    _____

2. The students are reading their books.

    _____

3. Ashur is careful not to burn himself while cooking.

    _____

Chapter 39
THE SUBJUNCTIVE MOOD

The **subjunctive** is the mood used to indicate a wish, hope, uncertainty or other comparable perspective toward a fact or an idea. For example:

> I wish you <u>could come</u> to the party.
>
> subjunctive mood of the verb *to come*

IN ENGLISH
The subjunctive is difficult to recognize because it is spelled like other tenses of the verb. It is used in two kinds of constructions.

1. The subjunctive is used in contrary-to-fact statements.

> If you *were* me, what would you do?
> - Implication: But you are not me.
>
> We wish that you were here.
> - Implication: But you aren't.

To negate this kind of subjunctive, simply add the word *not* after the subjunctive form of the verb.

> If I *did not* like cake so much, I'd be skinnier.
> If you *were not* visiting, I would go to work today.

1. The subjunctive is used in clauses following verbs of asking, wanting, telling, demanding or recommending.

> I asked that she *meet* me in my office.
> |
> instead of *meets*

> The judge ordered that he *be incarcerated.*
> |_____|
> instead of *is incarcerated*

These are just a few examples to show that English has the subjunctive mood, but it is not used as frequently as it is used in Swahili.

Note that these two sentences could also be written:

> *I asked her to meet me in my office.*
> *The judge ordered him to be incarcerated.*

These sentences still contain the subjunctive mood, although it is difficult to see. If the subject of the main verb in a sentence is different from the actor of the second verb, the second verb is in the subjunctive mood.

> I asked that she *meet* me in my office.
> **or**
> I asked her to *meet* me in my office.
> • *I* is the subject of the main verb, *asked.*
> • *She* is the actor of the second verb, *meet.*

To negate this kind of subjunctive, simply add the word *not* before the subjunctive verb.

> He asked her *not to come* to his house.
> **or**
> He asked that she *not come* to his house.

> They advised that I *not worry*.
> **or**
> They advised me *not to worry*.

KWA KISWAHILI

The subjunctive is called **dhamira tegemezi**. It is formed by combining the subject or object marker + dictionary form of the verb with the final *-a* changed to *-e*.

> **niende**   *I ought to go; let me go*
>   (from **kuenda**, *to go*)
> **wale**   *they ought to eat; let them eat*
>   (from **kula**, *to eat*)

Verbs that do not end in *-a* keep their final vowel.

> **ujibu**   *you ought to answer*
>   (from **kujibu**, *to answer*)
> **turudi**   *we ought to return; let's return*
>   (from **kurudi**, *to return*)

To negate the subjunctive, combine subject or object marker + negative marker *-si-* + dictionary form of the verb with the final *-a* changed to *-e*. Verbs that do not end in *-a* keep their final vowel.

nisiende *I shouldn't go; don't let me go*
wasile *they shouldn't eat; don't let them eat*
usijibu *you shouldn't answer; don't answer!*
tusirudi *we shouldn't return; let's not return*

The Swahili subjunctive is used in several kinds of constructions.

1. The subjunctive is used in clauses following verbs of asking, wanting, telling, demanding and recommending.

   Nilitaka *aje* nyumbani kwetu.
   I wanted <u>her to come</u> to our house.
   Nilitaka *asije* nyumbani kwetu.
   I wanted <u>her not to come</u> to our house.
   Aliomba *nimsaidie*.
   She asked <u>me to help her</u>.
   Aliomba *nisimsaidie*.
   She asked <u>me not to help her</u>.

As in English, you can tell that the subjunctive must be used if the subject of the first verb is different from the subject of the second verb.

2. The subjunctive is used to express commands that contain object markers. As explained in Chapter 34, if the object of the verb is a person, an object marker must be used.

   Nisaidie! *Help me!*
   Zichukue! *Take them!* (class 10)

To make this kind of command more polite, add the word **tafadhali** (*please*).

> **Tafadhali nisaidie!** *Please help me!*
> **Tafadhali zipate!** *Please get them!* (class 10)

3. The subjunctive is used to express negative commands.

> **Laila, usiende!** *Laila, don't go!*
> **Wanafunzi, msiende!** *Students, don't go!*

4. The subjunctive is used after **tafadhali** (*please*), **(ni) lazima** (*it is necessary*), **afadhali** (*it is better*) or **itabidi** (*it behooves*) to express a request or an obligation.

> **Ni lazima *uende*.** *You must go.*
>   (literally: *It is necessary that you go.*)
> **Lazima *tuende*.** *We must go.*
>   (literally: *It is necessary that we go.*)
> **Afadhali *tumwalike*.** *We'd better invite her.*
>   (literally: *It is better that we invite her.*)
> **Itabidi *msiende*.** *You all should not go.*
>   (literally: *It behooves you not to go.*)

5. The subjunctive is used to express the purpose of the action of a previous verb, after the word **ili** (*in order that*).

>   **Asome vitabu ili** *ajifunze.*
>   *He reads books in order to learn.*
>   **or**
>   *He reads books in order that he learn.*

6. The subjunctive is used to ask for permission.

>   *Nisome* **aya hii?**
>   *Am I to read this paragraph?*
>   *or*
>   *May I read this paragraph?*
>   *or*
>   *Should I read this paragraph?*

To make this kind of command more polite, add the word **tafadhali** (*please*).

>   **Tafadhali nisome aya hii?**
>   *May I please read this paragraph?*

7. The subjunctive is used to include the speaker in a command in the construction that means *let's*.

>   **Tuende.** *Let's go.*
>   **Tusifanye hivi.** *Let's not do this.*

TAKE NOTE

Note that because the subjunctive has so many uses in Swahili, and also because it can be formed with the subject or object marker, many constructions have more than one possible meaning.

Nisaidie.
- If **ni**- is the object, the meaning is *Help me!*
- If **ni**- is the subject, the meaning is *Let me help.*

To understand the intended meaning of a subjunctive construction, you will need to look at the context in which it occurs.

In Swahili the subjunctive mood is not used to express contrary-to-fact statements as it is in English. Contrary-to-fact statements in Swahili are expressed with the conditional mood, which is explained in Chapter 40.

REVIEW

Underline the subjunctive verb in each sentence.

1. I want him to help me with my homework.

2. He asked her to say her name again.

3. I wish that you could come.

4. He ordered that the food be brought immediately.

5. What do you want me to do?

Chapter 40
THE CONDITIONAL MOOD

The **conditional mood** is used to express the English words *should*, *could*, or *would*, as well as contrary-to-fact (unreal or implausible) statements.

past tense conditional mood of the verb **kuuliza** (*to ask*)

Ningelimwuliza lakini nilisahau.
I would have asked him but I forgot.

IN ENGLISH
There is no conditional mood. English uses the **indicative** and **subjunctive** moods to express *should*, *could*, *would*, and contrary-to-fact statements. You will learn more about contrary-to-fact statements in Chapter 51.

KWA KISWAHILI
The conditional mood is called **hali ya sharti**. It has two tenses: **present** and **past**.

PRESENT TENSE
The present tense is expressed by the morpheme -**nge**- after the subject marker and before the verb.

subject marker + -*nge*- + verb

Monosyllabic verbs use the verbal noun form of the verb to form the conditional mood.

ningekula *I would/could eat*

Polysyllabic verbs use the dictionary form of the verb to form the conditional mood.

tungeenda *we would/could go*

PAST TENSE
The past tense is expressed by the morpheme -**ngeli**- after the subject marker and before the verb.

subject marker + -*ngeli*- verb

Monosyllabic verbs use the verbal noun form of the verb to form the conditional mood.

ningelikula *I would/could/should have eaten*

Polysyllabic verbs use the dictionary form of the verb to form the conditional mood.

tungelienda *we would/could/should have gone*

TAKE NOTE

The conditional mood is most often used to express the English words *would* and *could*. In the past tense it may also express the word *should*.

Ungeliuliza kwanza.[13] *You should have asked first.*

Paying attention to context will help you determine whether Swahili words in the conditional mood express *could, should* or *would.*

---

[13] A saying from a **kanga**, a cloth with a Swahili proverb-like saying on it, worn by women throughout much of East Africa.

Chapter 41
VERB EXTENSIONS

While English verbs can change their meanings by changing their form or becoming compound verbs, Swahili verbs change their meanings by adopting verb extensions.

I ate breakfast.	*to eat* changes to
I made him eat breakfast.	*to make eat*

- single verb changes to a compound verb

Nilikula chamshakinywa.	*kula* (to eat)
	changes to
Nilimlisha chamshakinywa.	*kulisha* (to make eat)

- root verb takes a causative extension

KWA KISWAHILI
There are six different kinds of verb extensions, called **minyambuliko**: the **prepositional extension**, the **passive extension**, the **stative extension**, the **reciprocal extension**, the **causative extension**, and the **reversive extension**. They are added to the **root verb** or **kitenzi cha msingi**, to modify its meaning.

THE PREPOSITIONAL EXTENSION
This type of extension is called **mnyambuliko wa kufanyia** in Swahili. It is used to suggest that the action of the verb is done *to, for (on behalf of),* or *about* the direct object of the verb.

Nilimsomea.
I read to him.
Alinilipia.
He paid for me.
Tulikuzungumzia shule.
We talked to you about school.

A prepositional verb is formed by adding an extension to the verb. There are four forms of this extension: **-ia, -ea, -lia,** and **-lea.** Your textbook or teacher will explain how to know which form to use; for now you only need to be able to recognize the extension. When you see or hear a verb that ends in one of these forms, you will know that its meaning is prepositional. If you know the meaning of the root verb, the verb without any extensions, you will be able to figure out the meaning of the prepositional verb.

kufanyia *to do to/for* (from **kufanya,** *to do)*
kuendea *to go to/for* (from **kuenda,** *to go)*
kuzalia *to give birth to/for* (from **kuzaa,** *to give birth)*
kukojolea *to urinate on* (from **kukojoa,** *to urinate)*

Note that in English the object in these examples is the object of the preposition, but in Swahili it is a direct object. Whether the extension suggests the English preposition *to, for,* or *about* is determined by the meaning of the root verb and the context in which the verb is used.

THE PASSIVE EXTENSION
This type of extension is called **mnyambuliko wa kufanywa** in Swahili. It is used to suggest that the action of the verb is done to (rather than by) the subject of the verb; another actor is implied even if not directly stated.

Nilipigwa (na kaka yangu).
I was hit (by my brother).
Kilisomwa (na kamati).
It was read by the committee.
Aliambiwa (na daktari).
She was told (by the doctor).

A passive verb is formed by adding an extension to the verb. There are three forms of this extension: **-wa**, **-liwa**, and **-lewa**. Your textbook or teacher will explain how to know which form to use; for now you only need to be able to recognize the extension. When you see or hear a verb that ends in one of these forms, you will know that its meaning is passive. If you know the meaning of the root verb, the verb without any extensions, you will be able to figure out the meaning of the passive verb.

kuuzwa *to be sold* (from **kuuza**, *to sell*)
kujibiwa *to be answered* (from **kujibu**, *to answer*)
kununuliwa *to be bought* (from **kununua**, *to buy*)
kuolewa *to be married* (from **kuoa**, *to marry*)

You will learn more about passive verbs in Chapter 44.

THE STATIVE EXTENSION

This type of extension is called **mnyambuliko wa kufanyika** in Swahili. It is used to suggest that the action of the verb happens *to the subject*, but without an implied actor. It can also be used to suggest that the action of the verb is *able to happen*. For this reason, it is sometimes also called the *potential extension*.

Baisikeli ilivunjika. *The bicycle broke.*
Chakula kimeharibika. *The food is ruined.*
Inafanyika. *It is doable.*

When the stative extension is used to suggest that the action of the verb happens to the subject, the present tense is not used except to suggest that the action is still in the process of happening.

Baisikeli inavunjika. *The bicycle is breaking.*
Chakula kinaharibika. *The food is being ruined.*

The perfect tense, expressed by the -**me**- tense marker, is used instead if the result of the action is in the present.

Baisikeli imevunjika. *The bicycle is broken.*

A stative verb is formed by adding an extension to the verb. There are six forms of this extension: -**ika**, -**eka**, -**oka**, -**lika**, -**ikana** and -**ekana**. Your textbook or teacher will explain how to know which form to use; for now you only need to be able to recognize the extension. When you see or hear a verb that ends in one of these forms, you will know that its meaning is stative. If you know the meaning of the root verb, the verb without any extensions, you will be able to figure out the meaning of the stative verb.

kuvunjika *to be broken* (from **kuvunja**, *to break*)
kuendeka *to be passable* (from **kuenda**, *to go*)

> **kuondoka** *to leave* (from **kuondoa,** *to remove)*
> **kuchagulika** *to be chosen* (from **kuchagua,** *to choose)*
> **kusemekana** *to be said* (from **kusema,** *to say)*
> **kupatikana** *to be available* (from **kupata,** *to get)*

Since a stative verb has two possible meanings, either that the action of the verb happens to the subject or that the action of the verb is possible, you must know the meaning of the verb without its extension and listen to the context in which the extended verb occurs in order to decide which meaning is intended.

THE RECIPROCAL EXTENSION
This type of extension is called **mnyambuliko wa kufanyana** in Swahili. It is used to suggest that two or more subjects perform the action of the verb together or toward one another.

Tutaonana. *We will see each other.*
Wanapendana. *They love each other.*
Zilifanana. *They looked like each other.* (class 10)

Note that the subject of a reciprocal verb is usually plural, and there can be no object nor object infix.

A reciprocal verb is formed by adding an extension to the verb. There is only one form of this extension: **-ana**. For now you only need to be able to recognize the extension. When you see or hear a verb that ends in this form, you will know that its meaning is reciprocal. If you know the meaning of the root verb, the verb without any extensions, you will be able to figure out the meaning of the reciprocal verb.

kusikilizana *to listen to each other*
(from **kusikiliza**, *to listen to*)
kusaidiana *to help each other*
(from **kusaidia**, *to help*)

In some cases a reciprocal verb may take a singular subject if
the action is performed by a singular subject but reciprocated
by the object of the preposition (see Chapter 48). In this case
the verb is followed by the preposition *na*, which means *with*
or *and*, and then the object of the preposition.

Unafan<u>ana na</u> dada yako.
You look like your sister.
Nilikut<u>ana na</u> rais.
I met with the president.
Wazo lako linaend<u>ana na</u> mpango.
Your idea fits with the plan.

THE CAUSATIVE EXTENSION
This type of extension is called **mnyambuliko wa kufanyiza**
in Swahili. It is used to suggest that the subject causes the
direct object to perform the action of the verb.

Aliendesha gari. *He drove the car.*
(Literally: *He made the car go.*)
Pesa zako zilimwezesha asafiri.
Your money enabled him to travel.

The causative extension can also be used to turn an adjective
into a verb; the new verb suggests that the subject causes the
direct object to take on the attribute of the adjective.

sahihi *correct* ⟹	**kusahihisha** *to correct*
	(literally: *to make correct*)
bora *better/best* ⟹	**kuboresha** *to improve*
	(literally: *to make better*)
fupi *short* ⟹	**kufupisha** *to shorten*
	(literally: *to make short*)

In addition, the causative extension can be used to turn a noun into a verb.

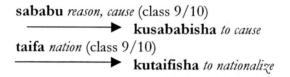

sababu *reason, cause* (class 9/10)
⟶ **kusababisha** *to cause*
taifa *nation* (class 9/10)
⟶ **kutaifisha** *to nationalize*

A causative verb is formed by adding an extension to the verb. There are six forms of this extension: **-isha, -esha, -lisha, -lesha, -iza** and **-eza.** Your textbook or teacher will explain how to know which form to use; for now you only need to be able to recognize the extension. When you see or hear a verb that ends in one of these forms, you will know that its meaning is causative. If you know the meaning of the root verb, the verb without any extensions, you will be able to figure out the meaning of the causative verb.

kuaminisha *to inspire confidence*
(from **kuamini**, *to believe*)
kuogopesha *to scare* (from **kuogopa**, *to fear*)
kukalisha *to seat* (from **kukaa**, *to sit*)
kuzoelesha *to train, teach*
(from **kuzoea**, *to get used to*)
kufanyiza *to cause* (from **kufanya**, *to do*)
kucheleza *to delay* (from **kuchelewa**, *to be late*)

THE REVERSIVE EXTENSION

This type of extension, also known as the *conversive extension* is called **mnyambuliko wa kufanyua** in Swahili. It is used to suggest the opposite or reverse of the root verb.

Nilifungua mlango. *I opened the door.*

A causative verb is formed by adding an extension to the verb. There is one form of this extension: **-ua**. Your textbook or teacher will explain how to use the extension; for now you only need to be able to recognize it. When you see or hear a verb that ends in this form, you will know that its meaning is causative. If you know the meaning of the root verb, the verb without any extensions, you will be able to figure out the meaning of the causative verb.

kufungua *to open* (from **kufunga**, *to close*)
kuvua *to undress* (from **kuvaa**, *to dress*)

MULTIPLE EXTENSIONS

Many verbs can take more than one extension in order to make their meanings even more complex. Here are a few examples.

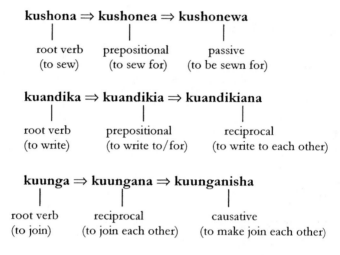

kushona ⇒ **kushonea** ⇒ **kushonewa**

root verb   prepositional   passive
(to sew)   (to sew for)   (to be sewn for)

kuandika ⇒ **kuandikia** ⇒ **kuandikiana**

root verb   prepositional   reciprocal
(to write)   (to write to/for)   (to write to each other)

kuunga ⇒ **kuungana** ⇒ **kuunganisha**

root verb   reciprocal   causative
(to join)   (to join each other)   (to make join each other)

TAKE NOTE

While a few dictionaries include entries for extended verbs, many do not. If you encounter an extended verb that is unfamiliar to you, you will need to learn to recognize (or make an educated guess at) the root verb so that you can find it in dictionaries.

When verb extensions are included in dictionaries, often these abbreviations are used:

prepositional	Prep.
passive	Ps.
stative	St. /Pot.
reciprocal	Rp.
causative	Cs.
reversive	Rv./Cv.

REVIEW

Using the root verb and its meaning,[14] indicate whether the extended verb is prepositional (Prep.), passive (Ps.), stative (St.), reciprocal (Rp.), causative (Cs.), or reversive (Rv.), and then give a possible English translation. Some verbs may have multiple extensions.

A. **kupinga** *to cause an obstruction, put in the way, obstruct, stop the way, block, thwart, check, oppose, contradict*

1. **kupingwa**   Prep   Ps   St   Rp   Cs   Rv

   Meaning: _____

2. **kupingika**   Prep   Ps   St   Rp   Cs   Rv

   Meaning: _____

3. **kupingia**   Prep   Ps   St   Rp   Cs   Rv

   Meaning: _____

4. **kupingisha**   Prep   Ps   St   Rp   Cs   Rv

   Meaning: _____

5. **kupingana**   Prep   Ps   St   Rp   Cs   Rv

   Meaning: _____

---

[14] The meanings given here are adapted from Frederick Johnson's *A Standard Swahili-English Dictionary* (1939. Nairobi & Dar es Salaam: Oxford U. P., 1999)

B. **kufuta** *to wipe, wipe out, wipe away, wipe off, clean up; to remove, obliterate, abolish, cause to be forgotten, erase*

1. **kufutwa**   Prep   Ps   St   Rp   Cs   Rv

    Meaning: _____

2. **kufutika**   Prep   Ps   St   Rp   Cs   Rv

    Meaning: _____

3. **kufutia**   Prep   Ps   St   Rp   Cs   Rv

    Meaning: _____

4. **kufutisha**   Prep   Ps   St   Rp   Cs   Rv

    Meaning: _____

5. **kufutana**   Prep   Ps   St   Rp   Cs   Rv

    Meaning: _____

C. **kupiga** *to strike, beat, hit, give a blow*

1. **kupigwa**   Prep   Ps   St   Rp   Cs   Rv

    Meaning: _____

2. **kupigika**   Prep   Ps   St   Rp   Cs   Rv

    Meaning: _____

3. **kupigia**   Prep   Ps   St   Rp   Cs   Rv

    Meaning: _____

4. **kupigisha**   Prep   Ps   St   Rp   Cs   Rv

    Meaning: _____

5. **kupigana**   Prep   Ps   St   Rp   Cs   Rv

   Meaning: _____

6. **kupiganisha**   Prep   Ps   St   Rp   Cs   Rv

   Meaning: _____

Chapter 42
PARTICIPLES

A **participle** is a verb used as an adjective or as part of a compound verb.

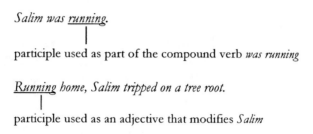

Salim was _running_.

|

participle used as part of the compound verb _was running_

Running home, Salim tripped on a tree root.

|

participle used as an adjective that modifies _Salim_

IN ENGLISH
A participle is the _-ing_ form of a verb.

coming _going_ _sitting_

The participle has three functions:

1. as part of a verb phrase to form the progressive forms (see Chapter 43, Compound Tenses).

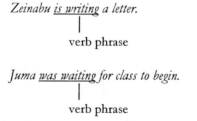

Zeinabu _is writing_ a letter.

|

verb phrase

Juma _was waiting_ for class to begin.

|

verb phrase

2. as an adjective to describe a noun or pronoun (see Chapter 15, _Descriptive Adjectives_). In this function it is known as a **gerundive.**

Zeinabu is a <u>loving</u> woman.

adjective describing the noun *woman*

She is <u>interesting</u>.

adjective describing the pronoun *she*

3. as an adjective introducing a participial phrase. In this function it is known as a **gerundive.** As an adjective, it can modify any noun in a sentence.

>   I went to the store *carrying* a bag.
>   - The entire phrase *carrying a bag* functions as an adjective modifying the subject, *I.*

>   *Walking* to school, Rajabu saw a snake.
>   - The entire phrase *walking to school* is an adjective modifying the subject, *Rajabu.*

>   Sudi saw the teacher *smiling.*
>   - *Smiling* is an adjective modifying the object, *teacher.*

KWA KISWAHILI

The participle in Swahili is called a ***tenseless participle*** or **kitenzi cha -ki-.** The plural, ***tenseless participles***, is called **vitenzi vya -ki-.** It is formed by combining a subject marker + the infix *-**ki**-* + the dictionary form of the verb. Because a subject marker is included, and because it functions as an adjective, the Swahili tenseless participle must agree in class with the noun or pronoun it modifies.

>   **nikienda** *I going*
>   **wakija** *they coming*
>   **tukikaa** *we sitting*

The participle has two functions:

1. as part of a verb phrase to form the past and future progressive forms (see Chapter 43, Compound Tenses).

   past progressive
   |

   Mosi <u>alikuwa akifanya</u> mazoezi.
   Mosi was doing exercises.

   future progressive
   |

   <u>Utakuwa ukisoma</u> leo jioni.
   You will be studying this evening.

2. as an adjective introducing a participial phrase. In this function it is known as a **kivumishijina**. As an adjective, it can modify any noun in a sentence.

   Nilienda dukani *nikibeba* mfuko.
   I went to the store carrying a bag.
   - *Nikibeba* is an adjective modifying the first person singular subject, indicated by the subject prefix ***ni-***.
   - The participial phrase is **nikibeba mfuko**.

Akitembea kuelekea shuleni, Rajabu aliona
nyoka.
Walking to school, Rajabu saw a snake.

- *Akitembea* is an adjective modifying the
  third person singular subject, indicated by the
  subject prefix *a-* and the pronoun *Rajabu*.
- The participial phrase is *Akitembea
  kuelekea shuleni*.

Sudi alimwona mwalimu *akitabasamu*.
Sudi saw the teacher smiling.

- *Akitabasamu* is an adjective modifying the
  third person singular object, indicated by the
  subject prefix *a-* and the noun *mwalimu*.

TAKE NOTE

What might appear to be a present participle (verbal adjective
or gerundive) because it is a verb form ending in *-ing* could
also be a **gerund** (verbal noun). Be sure to read Chapter 4,
Verbal Nouns, in which there is a chart summarizing the
various English *-ing* forms and their Swahili equivalents.

REVIEW

Underline the participles in the sentences below. For each sentence, circle whether the participle is used as an adjective (A) or as part of a verb phrase (VP).

1. Musa was walking to the store.   A   VP

2. Mariamu, studying for her exam,
   was tired.   A   VP

3. Learning the students' names, the
   teacher felt overwhelmed.   A   VP

4. What will you be doing?   A   VP

5. This morning we were cooking breakfast
   when there was a knock at the door.   A   VP

Chapter 43
COMPOUND TENSES

Compound tenses are used to create verb tenses that are more complex than those that are considered "simple."

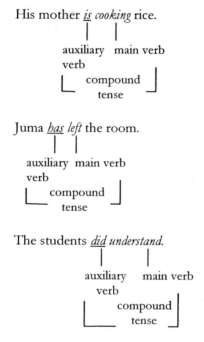

His mother *is cooking* rice.
| |
auxiliary main verb
verb
compound
tense

Juma *has left* the room.
| |
auxiliary main verb
verb
compound
tense

The students *did understand.*
| |
auxiliary main verb
verb
compound
tense

IN ENGLISH

In English these are the simple and compound tenses, conjugated here in the first person singular:

SIMPLE	**present**	*I go*
TENSES	**past**	*I went*
	future	*I will go*
	perfect	*I have gone*
	past perfect	*I had gone*
	future perfect	*I will have gone*

COMPOUND	**perfect progressive**	I have been going
TENSES	**past progressive**	I was going
	past perfect progressive	I had been going
	future progressive	I will be going
	future perfect progressive	I will have been going

Simple tenses are explained in Chapters 21-29.

As you can see in the above examples, compound tenses in English have a progressive meaning. To create compound tenses in English, auxiliary verbs and the present participle are used. *Have, has, be, been, was, had,* and *will* are all examples of **auxiliary verbs**, verbs that help the main verb.

To make the perfect tense progressive, the subject, the verb, and two auxiliary verbs combine in this way:

subject + have/has + been + tenseless participle

It has been raining.
They have been planting maize.

To make the past tense progressive, the subject, the verb, and one auxiliary verb combine in this way:

subject + was/were + tenseless participle

She was resting. *We were working.*

To make the past perfect tense progressive, the subject, the verb, and two auxiliary verbs combine in this way:

subject + had + been + tenseless participle

They had been working for an hour when the machine broke.

To make the future tense progressive, the subject, the verb, and two auxiliary verbs combine in this way:

subject + will + be + tenseless participle

You all will be eating at 2 o'clock.

To make the future perfect tense progressive, the subject, the verb and two auxiliary verbs combine in this way:

subject + will + have + past participle

You will have mastered Swahili grammar when you finish this book.

KWA KISWAHILI

In Swahili compound tenses are called **tensi za maneno mawili**, which literally means *two-word tenses.*

These are the two-word tenses, conjugated here in the first person singular.

PERFECT PROGRESSIVE   **nimekuwa nikienda**
                             I have been going
PAST PROGRESSIVE   **nilikuwa nikienda**
                             I was going
PAST PERFECT   **nilikuwa nimeenda**
                             I had gone
FUTURE PROGRESSIVE   **nitakuwa nikienda**
                             I will be going
FUTURE PERFECT   **nitakuwa nimeenda**
                             I will have gone

Note that two of the tenses that are considered "simple" in English are compound tenses in Swahili: the past perfect and the future perfect. Swahili compound tenses can have a progressive or a perfect meaning.

Two of the tenses that are compound in English are actually three-word tenses, **tensi za maneno matatu,** in Swahili.

PAST PERFECT PROGRESSIVE
       nilikuwa nimekuwa nikienda
       I had been going

FUTURE PERFECT PROGRESSIVE
nitakuwa nimekuwa nikienda
I will have been going

As you can see, to create compound tenses in Swahili, the verb **kuwa** (to be) and the tenseless participle are used. The verb **kuwa** functions as an **auxiliary verb**, a verb that help the main verb.   The conjugation of the verb **kuwa** is explained in Chapter 30.

To make the perfect tense progressive, the verb **kuwa** and the tenseless participle combine in this way:

perfect tense of *kuwa* + tenseless participle

Mvua <u>imekuwa ikinyesha</u>.
It has been raining.

To make the past tense progressive, the verb **kuwa** and the tenseless participle combine in this way:

past tense of *kuwa* + tenseless participle

Alikuwa akipumzika. *She was resting.*

To make the future tense progressive, the verb **kuwa** and the tenseless participle combine in this way:

future tense of *kuwa* + tenseless participle

<u>Mtakuwa mkila</u> saa nane.
You all will be eating at 2 o'clock.

To make the past tense perfect, the verb **kuwa** and the main verb combine in this way:

> past tense of *kuwa* + perfect tense of the main verb

Tulikuwa tumesoma. *We had studied.*

To make the future tense perfect, the verb **kuwa** and the main verb combine in this way:

> future tense of *kuwa* + perfect tense of the main verb

Nyumba <u>itakuwa imejengwa</u>.
The house will have been built.

To make the past perfect tense progressive, the verb **kuwa** and the main verb combine in this way:

> past tense of *kuwa* + perfect tense of *kuwa* + tenseless participle

Walikuwa wamekuwa wakizungumza.
They had been talking.

To make the future perfect tense progressive, the verb **kuwa** and the main verb combine in this way:

> future tense of *kuwa* + perfect tense of *kuwa* + tenseless participle

Tutakuwa tumekuwa tukisafiri.
We will have been travelling.

REVIEW

Read the following paragraph. Underline the phrases that make up a compound tense in English. Make a list of those phrases that would require a compound tense in Swahili, and give the name of the compound tense.

One afternoon Zakia was walking in the woods. She had woken up early that morning so by the afternoon she had grown quite tired. "When will I reach the lake?" she was wondering. "Will I be walking all day? By the time I arrive, it will have grown dark."

Swahili Compound Tense	Name
1. _____	_____
2. _____	_____
3. _____	_____
4. _____	_____
5. _____	_____
6. _____	_____

Chapter 44
ACTIVE AND PASSIVE VOICE

The voice of the verb refers to the relationship between the subject of the verb and the action that the verb expresses. There are two voices: active and passive.

A sentence is in the **active voice** when the verb indicates an action performed by the subject. A verb in the active voice is called an **active verb.**

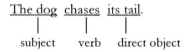

In this example, the subject, *the dog,* performs the action of the verb, *chases,* and the direct object, *its tail,* is the recipient of the action.

A sentence is in the **passive voice** when the verb indicates the action done to the subject by someone or something else. A verb in the passive voice is called a **passive verb.**

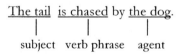

In this example, the subject, *the tail,* does not perform the action of the verb, *is chased,* but rather is having the action of the verb performed upon it. The doer of the action, *the dog,* is called the **agent.**

IN ENGLISH

The passive voices is expressed by the verb *to be* conjugated in the proper tense + the past participle of the main verb. Note that the tense of the sentence is indicated by the tense of the auxiliary verb *to be*.

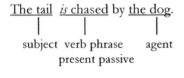

The tail *is* chased by the dog.
| | | |
subject   verb phrase   agent
            present passive

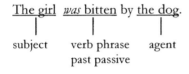

The girl *was* bitten by the dog.
| | | |
subject   verb phrase   agent
            past passive

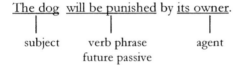

The dog will be punished by its owner.
| | | |
subject   verb phrase   agent
            future passive

KWA KISWAHILI

The active voice is called **sauti ya kufanya** and the passive voice is **sauti ya fanywa**. Likewise an active verb is called **kitenzi cha kufanya** and a passive verb is **kitenzi cha kufanywa.**

Passive verbs are not expressed with an auxiliary verb. Instead, the passsive is expressed by a **passive extension** or **mnyambuliko wa kufanywa**, which is added to the end of the root verb. You learned about the passive extension in Chapter 41 (Verb Extensions).

The basic passive ending is -**wa,** but depending on the vowel sounds in the root verb, it may occur as -**wa,** -**liwa,** and -**lewa.** Your teacher or textbook will explain how to choose the proper ending when forming a passive verb; for now you only need to know how to recognize the passive.

A passive verb can be used in any tense.

PRESENT	**anaambiwa/aambiwa** *she is told/she is being told*
PERFECT	**ameambiwa** *she has been told*
PAST	**aliambiwa** *she was told*
FUTURE	**ataambiwa** *she will be told*
PERFECT PROGRESSIVE	**amekuwa akiambiwa** *she has been being told*[*]
PAST PROGRESSIVE	**alikuwa akiambiwa** *she was being told*
PAST PERFECT	**alikuwa ameambiwa** *she had been told*
FUTURE PROGRESSIVE	**atakuwa akiambiwa** *she will be being told*[*]
FUTURE PERFECT	**atakuwa ameambiwa** *she will have been told*
PAST PERFECT PROGRESSIVE	**alikuwa amekuwa akiambiwa** *she has been being told*[*]

[*] Note that some of these constructions would not occur in English; nevertheless the Swahili forms may exist.

FUTURE PERFECT PROGRESSIVE	**atakuwa amekuwa akiambiwa** *she will have been being told**

In Swahili the **agent**, which is called **wakala** or **ajenti**, is expressed in one of two ways depending on whether it is a living being (i.e. a person or an animal) or a non-living thing (i.e. an object or idea).

When the agent is a person or animal, the passive verb is followed by the preposition **na**, and then the agent. **Na** in this case means *by*, but in other situations it may also mean *with* or *and*.

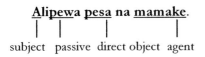

<u>Alipewa</u> <u>pesa</u> na <u>mamake</u>.

    subject   passive   direct object   agent

(He was given money by his mother.)

When the agent is a non-living thing, the passive verb is followed by the preposition **kwa**, and then the agent. **Kwa** in this case means *by* or *with*, but in other situations it may also mean *for* or *to*.

---

* Note that some of these constructions would not occur in English; nevertheless the Swahili forms may exist.

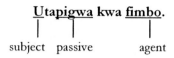

subject   passive   agent

(You will be hit with a stick.)

TAKE NOTE

A passive Swahili verb <u>never</u> takes an object marker.

REVIEW

Underline the verb or the verb phrase in each of the sentences below. Circle whether each verb is active (A) or passive (P). You should be able to identify the verb in each Swahili sentence even if you don't know what the sentence means. If you can't identify a Swahili verb, you should reread Chapter 21 (Introduction to Verbs and Verb Tenses).

1.	*The books were moved yesterday.*	A	P
2.	*Akia moved the books this morning.*	A	P
3.	*Was she hurt?*	A	P
4.	*No, she didn't hurt herself.*	A	P
5.	*When will she sell the books?*	A	P
6.	**Vitabu vitauzwa kesho asubuhi.**	A	P
7.	**Kwa nini aliamua kuuza vitabu vyake?**	A	P
8.	**Aliamrishwa na babake.**	A	P
9.	**Je, watu wengi watanunua vitabu?**	A	P
10.	**Ndiyo; vitabu vitanunuliwa na mashule.**	A	P

ADVERBS

Chapter 45
ADVERBS

An **adverb** is a word that describes a verb, an adjective or another adverb. Adverbs indicate manner, quantity, time, place and intensity.

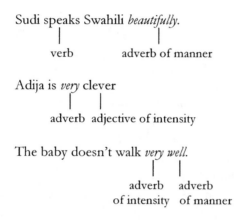

IN ENGLISH

Adverbs can describe verbs, adjectives or other adverbs in a variety of ways.

♦ **Adverbs of manner** answer the question *how*. They are very common adverbs and can usually be recognized by their suffix *-ly*.

The rabbit ran *quickly*.
- *Quickly* describes the verb *ran;* it tells you how the rabbit ran.

♦ **Adverbs of quantity, degree or intensity** answer the question *how much* or *how well.*

> The rabbit ran *often.*
> > • *Often* describes the verb *ran;* it tells you how much the rabbit ran.

♦ **Adverbs of time** answer the question *when.*

> The rabbit will run *soon.*
> > • *Soon* describes the verb *will run;* it tells you when the rabbit will run.

♦ **Adverbs of place** answer the question *where.*

> The rabbit is running *around.*
> > • *Around* describes the verb *is running;* it tells you where the rabbit is running.

KWA KISWAHILI
Adverbs, called **vielezi** in Swahili, are invariable; they never change form.

Swahili adverbs have the same functions as English adverbs.

vielezi vya jinsi	*adverbs of manner*
vielezi vya kadiri	*adverbs of degree or intensity*
vielezi vya hesabu	*adverbs of quantity*
vielezi vya wakati	*adverbs of time*
vielezi vya mahali	*adverbs of place*

Some adverbs are formed from the adjective stems plus the class 8 adjectival prefix **vi-**. Almost any adjective stem can be turned into an adverb.

Juma anacheza mpira <u>vizuri</u>.
Juma plays soccer <u>well</u>.
- **Vizuri** is formed from the adjective stem
  -zuri *(good, well)*.

One adverb that is formed from an adjective stem in a different way is **kidogo** *(a little)*, from the stem **-dogo** *(small)*. It takes the class 7 adjectival prefix **-ki**.

Ninampenda <u>kidogo</u>. *I like him <u>a little</u>.*

Some adverbs are formed by combining **kwa** + abstract nouns.

Juma alitembea <u>kwa haraka</u>.
Juma walked <u>quickly</u>.
- **Kwa haraka** is formed from the noun **haraka** *(speed)*.

Adverbs that refer to styles associated with ethnic groups or nationalities are formed from the class 1 nouns by replacing the class 1 noun prefix with the class 7 adjective prefix. They are always capitalized. (Don't confuse these forms with the nouns used to refer to languages, such as **Kiswahili** and **Kiingereza**.)

Mzungu *(a European)* ⇒ **Kizungu** *(in a European style)*
Mswahili *(a Swahili)* ⇒ **Kiswahili** *(in a Swahili style)*

TAKE NOTE

In English some adverbs are identical in form to the corresponding adjectives.

Juma is *fast.*	Juma runs *fast.*
adjective	adverb
modifies the noun *Juma*	modifies the verb *run*

It is important that you differentiate between a word used as an adverb or as an adjective so that, if you are translating into Swahili, you will know which Swahili form to use: the adverb, which is invariable; or the adjective, which agrees in class with the noun it modifes.

REVIEW

A. Circle the adverbs in the sentences below, and underline the word each adverb modifies. Circle the part of speech of the word the adverb modifies: verb (V), adjective (Adj.), or adverb (Adv.).

1. Kezilihabi writes beautifully.

    V   Adj.   Adv.

2. His novels are very interesting.

    V   Adj.   Adv.

3. *Rosa Mistika* is worth reading often.

    V   Adj.   Adv.

4. The main character, Rosa, is quite sympathetic.

    V   Adj.   Adv.

5. You will feel extremely sorry for her.

    V   Adj.   Adv.

B. Circle whether the underlined word in each of the sentences below is an adjective (Adj.) or an adverb (Adv.).

1. **Viatu hivi ni <u>vizuri</u>.**   Adj.   Adv.

2. **Tunafahamiana <u>vizuri</u>.**   Adj.   Adv.

3. **Vitendo vyake vilikuwa <u>vibaya</u>.**   Adj.   Adv.

4. **Timu yetu ilicheza <u>vibaya</u>.**   Adj.   Adv.

5. **Anavaa <u>Kimarekani</u>.**   Adj.   Adv.

CONJUNCTIONS

Chapter 46
CONJUNCTIONS

A **conjunction** is a word that joins words or groups of words.

> Adija *and* her mother are having an argument.
> *Neither* Sudi *nor* Zuhura eat meat.
> I wanted to go to the party, *but* I was sick.

IN ENGLISH
There are two kinds of conjunctions: **coordinating** and **subordinating**.

Coordinating conjunctions join words, phrases, and clauses that are equal in form; they connect or *coordinate* ideas of equal rank. Typical coordinating conjunctions are *and, but, or, nor, yet,* and *for.*

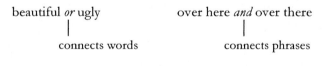

    beautiful *or* ugly   over here *and* over there
          | |
    connects words   connects phrases

    The day was warm *but* we felt comfortable.
                      |
              connects clauses

Subordinating conjunctions join a dependent clause to a main clause; they subordinate one clause to another. The main idea is expressed in the main clause, and the clause introduced by a subordinating conjunction is called a subordinate clause. Typical subordinate conjunctions are *although, because, if, unless, so that, while, that, whenever,* and *until.*

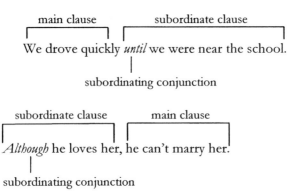

NOTE: The main clause is not always the first clause of the sentence.

KWA KISWAHILI
Conjunctions, called **viunganishi** in Swahili, are invariable; they never change. They do not have number, class or tense.

The major coordinating conjunctions are **na** *(and)*, **lakini** *(but)*, **au** *(or)*, and **wala** *(nor)*. Typical subordinating conjunctions are **ijapo** *(although)*, **ingawa** *(although)*, **kwa sababu** *(because)*, **kwani** *(because)*, **kwa kuwa** *(because)*, **kama** *(if)*, **wakati** *(when)*, **ili** *(so that)*, **kabla** *(before)* and **baada** *(after)*.

Most conjunctions require the use of the indicative mood (in any tense) for the verb that follows.

> **Ataenda dukani <u>kwa sababu anahitaji</u> sukari.**
> *She will go to the store <u>because she needs</u> sugar.*

However, there are a few exceptions. **Ili** *(so that)* requires the use of the subjunctive mood for the verb that follows.

> **Nilikuambia <u>ili ujue</u>.**
> *I told you <u>so that you'd know</u>.*

Wakati *(when)* requires the use of the relative construction with the class 16 relative infix -**po**- in the verb that follows.

> **<u>Wakati nilipoenda</u> shuleni, nilikuwa mdogo.**
> *<u>When I went</u> to school, I was small.*

Kabla *(before)* requires the use of the negative imperfect tense in the verb that follows.

> **<u>Kabla hajafika</u>, tuliwazungumzia watoto wetu.**
> *<u>Before he arrived</u>, we talked about our children.*

Baada *(after)* requires the use of the imperfect tense in the verb that follows.

> **<u>Baada amefika</u>, tuliacha kuwazungumzia watoto wetu.**
> *<u>After he arrived</u>, we stopped talking about our children.*

Kama *(if)* requires the use of the conditional tense in the verb that follows.

> <u>**Kama akija, tutamwona.**</u>
> <u>*If he comes, we will see him.*</u>

When you learn a new conjunction, be sure to memorize what kind of verb it governs.

Subordinating Conjunction or Preposition?

Occasionally the same word can be used as a subordinating conjunction and a preposition in English. Some of the Swahili subordinating conjunctions are also used as prepositions, but with slight modifications.

For instance, *before* can be used as a subordinating conjunction and as a preposition in English. In Swahili, however, as a subordinating conjunction *before* is **kabla**, but **kabla ya** as a preposition. The subordinating conjunction **wakati** *(when)* becomes **wakati wa** as a preposition, and the subordinating conjunction **baada** *(after)* becomes **baada ya** as a preposition.

You can distinguish between a preposition and a subordinating conjunction simply by determining if the word introduces a prepositional phrase or a subordinate clause (see Chapter 47).

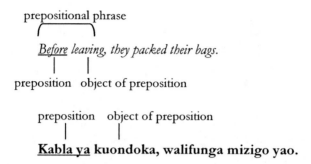

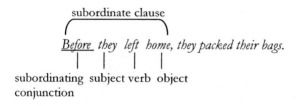

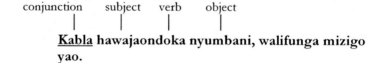

REVIEW

In the sentences below, circle whether the underlined word is a preposition (P) or a subordinate conjunction (SC).

1. I spoke to him <u>after</u> class.

    P   SC

2. <u>After</u> you finish reading, write out a summary.

    P   SC

3. I believed him <u>because</u> I know he is an honest person.

    P   SC

4. <u>Because</u> of her illness, she was unable to attend.

    P   SC

5. She read the book <u>before</u> she saw the movie.

    P   SC

6. We met up <u>before</u> the party.

    P   SC

PREPOSITIONS

Chapter 47
PREPOSITIONS & PREPOSITIONAL PHRASES

A **preposition** is a word that shows the relationship between a noun or pronoun and another word in the sentence. Prepositions may indicate position, direction, time, manner, means or agent.

I walked <u>by</u> the store.

preposition of direction

Juma was given a gift <u>by</u> his teacher.

preposition of agent

IN ENGLISH
The noun or pronoun that the preposition connects to the rest of the sentence is called the **object of the preposition**. Together they make up a **prepositional phrase**. Here are examples of prepositional phrases.

- to show location   The book is *<u>on</u> the table.*

- to show direction   Come *<u>toward</u> me.*

- to show time   She has studied Swahili *<u>for</u> years.*

- to show manner   He ate the meal *<u>with</u> great fervor.*

- to show means   I cut myself *with the knife.*

- to show agent   The show was seen *by
                         many.*

To help you recognize prepositional phrases, here is a passage in which the prepositional phrases are in italics and the preposition that introduces each phrase is underlined.

Africa is the second-largest continent (*after Asia*), straddling the equator and lying largely *within the tropics.* Africa forms a plateau *between the Atlantic and Indian oceans. Before the 1880s* Europeans were, except *in South Africa,* largely confined *to the coastal regions. By the end of the 19th century* the whole continent, *except for Liberia and Ethiopia,* was under foreign domination either *by European powers* or *by the Ottoman Empire.* Beginning *in the 1949s,* the former colonies secured their independence *within the space of 40 years,* but the process *of rapid decolonization* brought unrest and instability *to many parts of the continent.* A major factor *in this unrest* was, and continues to be, the artificial boundaries created *by colonialism.*[15]

---

[15] Quoted from "Africa," *Oxford One-Volume Illustrated Encyclopedia* (London: Oxford, 1997).

KWA KISWAHILI

Prepositions are called **vihusishi**. The noun or pronoun that the preposition connects to the rest of the sentence is called the **shamirisho ya kihusishi**. Together they make up a **kirai cha kihusishi**. There are several uses of prepositions in Swahili.

- to show location

    Alikaa *chini* ya mti.
    *She sat **under** the tree.*

- to show time

    Tulikuja *kabla ya* saa tatu.
    *We came **before** nine o'clock*

- to show cause

    Alipigwa *kwa sababu ya* makosa.
    *He was beaten **because of mistakes**.*

- to show agent

    Alipewa zawadi *na* mama yake.
    *She was given a gift **by her mother**.*

- to show means[16]

    Alikatwa *kwa* kisu.
    *She was cut **by a knife**.*

---

[16] Note that when a passive verb is followed by a preposition of agent and the object of the preposition is animate, the preposition is *na;* but when it is followed by a preposition of means and the object of the preposition is inanimate, the preposition is *kwa*. See Chapter 44, Active and Passive Voice.

- to show possession   **Nipe kitabu _cha_ Sudi.**
  Give me <u>Sudi's</u> book.
  (Literally: *the book <u>of Sudi</u>.*)

- to show type   **Amevaa nguo _za_ Kiunguja.**
  He is wearing <u>Zanzibari</u> clothing.[17]
  (Literally: <u>*of the Zanzibari style*</u>.)

- to show manner   **Alisema _kwa_ ukali.**
  She spoke <u>severely</u>.[18]
  (Literally: <u>**with/by**</u> *severity*.)

- to show comparison   **Adija anasoma zaidi _kuliko_ Sudi.**
  *Adija studies more **than** Sudi.*

---

[17] Note that prepositions that show type form prepositional phrases that function as adjectives. See Chapter 14, Adjectives.

[18] Note that prepositions that show manner form prepositional phrases that function as adverbs. See Chapter 45, Adverbs.

TAKE NOTE

You must learn to distinguish in English between prepositional phrases introduced by *to* indicating the indirect object (see Chapter 36, Indirect Objects) and *to* indicating direction toward a location, because these take different forms in Swahili.

♦   *to* indicating a direct object ⇒ *prepositional verb*

> The action of the verb is done to or for someone or something. The prepositional phrase answers the question *to what?* or *to whom?* In English, the indirect object can be expressed either by *to* or by reversing the word order and putting the indirect object without the *to* before the direct object (see Chapter 34, Objects).

> He read the book **to** *me*.
> He read *me* the book.
> - He read the book to whom? To me.
> - *Me* is the indirect object.

> In Swahili, the indirect object must be expressed as the object of a prepositional verb.

> **Ali<u>ni</u>som<u>ea</u> kitabu.** *He read the book* **to me.**

♦   *to* indicating direction toward a location ⇒ **kuelekea** + object

> The preposition *to* is used in a phrase of direction towards a location. It answers the question *to where?*

> She was running **to** *school*.
> - She was running to where? To school.

- *To school* is the object of the preposition *to*.

In Swahili, if the object of the preposition is an object, the locative is expressed by the infinitive of the verb **kuelekea** (*to go toward*) + a class 17 noun.

Alikuwa akikimbia *kuelekea shuleni*.
*She was running **toward** the school.*

If the object of the preposition is animate, the locative is expressed by the infinitive of the verb **kuelekea** + the noun.

Alikuwa akikimbia *kunielekea* mimi.
*She was running **toward** me.*

REVIEW

Underline the prepositional phrases in the sentences below,[19] and circle the prepositions.

1. The United Republic of Tanzania consists of the mainland republic of Tanganyika and the island republic of Zanzibar.

2. The interior is dominated by a plateau.

3. The capital, Dodoma, lies in the center of Tanzania.

4. The plateau is broken by the Great Rift Valley, the west arm of which contains lake Tanganyika.

5. The east arm runs through central Tanzania to meet the west arm near Lake Malawi.

---

[19] Quoted from "Tanzania," *Oxford One-Volume Illustrated Encyclopedia* (London: Oxford, 1997).

Chapter 48
OBJECT OF THE PREPOSITION

An **object of a preposition** is a noun or pronoun which receives the action of the verb through a preposition.

I walked by <u>the store</u>.

object of the preposition *by*

Juma carried a gift for <u>his teacher</u>.

object of the preposition *for*

IN ENGLISH

An object of a preposition receives the action of the verb through a preposition other than *to*. (Objects of the preposition *to* are considered indirect objects and are discussed in Chapter 36.) It answers the question *whom?* or *what?* asked after the preposition.

Sudi is shopping *for new shoes.*

- Sudi is shopping for what? New shoes.
- *New shoes* is the object of the preposition *for.*

I went to the game *with my father.*

- I went to the game with whom? My father.
- *My father* is the object of the preposition *with.*

KWA KISWAHILI

An object of a preposition, called **shamirisho ya kihusishi** in Swahili, receives the action of the verb through any preposition. (Prepositions are explained in Chapter 47.) It answers the question **nani?** *(who?)* or **nini?** *(what?)* asked after the preposition.

> **Alizungumza *na mwenyeduka*.**
> *He spoke <u>with the shopkeeper</u>.*
> - **Alizungumza na nani? Mwenyeduka.**

> **Tulisafiri *kwa basi*.** *We travelled <u>by bus</u>.*
> - **Tulisafiri kwa nini? Basi.**

TAKE NOTE

The relationship between a verb and its object is often different in English and Swahili. For example, a verb may take an object of a preposition in English but a direct object in Swahili. Therefore, when you learn a Swahili verb it is important to find out if its meaning incorporates a preposition. Your textbook and dictionaries will indicate when the meaning of a Swahili verb incorporates a preposition.

ENGLISH: object of a preposition
⇒ SWAHILI: direct object

He is looking *for coffee*.

- Function in English: object of a preposition
- *He is looking for what? Coffee.*
- *Coffee* is the object of the preposition *for*.

Anatafuta kahawa.

- Function in Swahili: direct object
- **Anatafuta nini? Kahawa.**
- The verb **kutafuta** is not followed by a preposition; therefore, its object is a direct object.

Many common verbs require an object of a preposition in English, but a direct object in Swahili, because their meanings already incorporate a preposition.

to look at	**kuangalia**
to wait for	**kusubiri**

An object of one of these verbs, or of a prepositional verb (explained in Chapter 41, Verb Extensions), is not an object of a preposition; it is an object or an indirect object.

REVIEW

Circle the object of the preposition in each sentence.

1. They will walk by the window.

2. I went to the store for Zawadi.

3. The oranges were sold in bunches.

4. The teacher told us about Swahili grammar.

5. Let's speak in a whisper.

SENTENCES

Chapter 49
SENTENCES, PHRASES & CLAUSES

A **sentence** is the expression of a complete thought. For example:

> *The dog ran across the street.*

A **phrase** is a group of two or more words expressing a thought, but without a subject or a conjugated verb; it may contain an object.

> *the dog*   *across <u>the street</u>*
>
> object of the preposition *across*

A **clause** is a group of words containing a subject and a conjugated verb.

> *the dog ran*
> *he saw a cat*

A clause can combine with other clauses to form a compound or complex sentence.

> *The dog ran across the street because he saw a cat.*

IN ENGLISH
<u>SENTENCES</u>
A **sentence** usually consists of at least of a subject (see Chapter 19) and a verb (see Chapter 21).

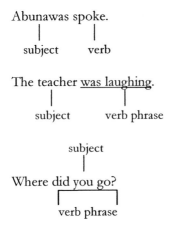

Depending on the verb, a sentence may also have **direct** and **indirect objects** (see Chapters 35-36).

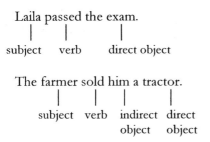

In addition, a sentence may include various kinds of **modifiers**: **adjectives** (see Chapter 14), **adverbs** (see Chapter 45), **prepositional phrases** (see Chapter 47), and **participial phrases** (see Chapter 42). Modifiers are adjectival if they modify nouns. Modifiers are adverbial if they modify verbs, adjectives or adverbs.

Laila passed the *difficult* exam.
|
adjective

Laila *successfully* passed the exam.
|
adverb

Laila passed the exam *despite her refusal to study*.
|
adverbial prepositional phrase
telling how Laila passed

Laila, *trying hard to remember details*, passed the exam.
|
adjectival participial phrase modifying Laila

It is important that you be able to recognize complete sentences and to distinguish phrases and clauses from complete sentences.

PHRASES
The various kinds of phrases are identified by the type of word beginning the phrase.

1. **prepositional phrase**: a preposition + object of preposition

    along the road   *after* the party
    towards the house

A prepositional phrase is adjectival if it modifies a noun, adverbial if it modifies a verb. (See Chapter 47, Prepositions, and Chapter 48, Object of the Preposition.)

2. **participial phrase**: starts with a participle

A participial phrase is adjectival since it modifies a noun.
(See Chapter 42, Participles.)

3. **infinitive phrase**: starts with an infinitive

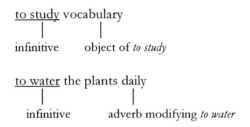

4. **verb phrase**: starts with an auxiliary verb or word (see
Chapter 33)

To recognize such phrases you need to recognize the
individual parts (prepositions, participles, infinitives) and
then isolate all those words within groups of words which
work as a unit of meaning. If this unit of meaning does
not have both a subject and a conjugated verb, it is a
phrase.

CLAUSES

There are two kinds of clauses: **main** (or **independent**) and **subordinate** (or **dependent**). A **main clause** generally expresses a complete thought, the important idea of the sentence. If it stood alone with a capitalized first word and a period at the end, it could be a simple sentence. A **subordinate clause** cannot stand alone as a complete sentence. It must always be combined with a main clause.

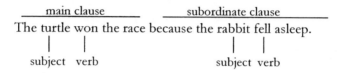

```
      main clause              subordinate clause
The turtle won the race because the rabbit fell asleep.
      |      |                        |      |
   subject  verb                   subject verb
```

TYPES OF SENTENCES

There are three types of sentences: **simple, compound,** and **complex**.

1. A **simple sentence** consists of only one main clause with no subordinate clauses. It has a subject and a conjugated verb. There may be many modifiers with a variety of word order.

    There is no set position for the verb in an English sentence or clause, but the subject usually comes before the verb, except in questions.

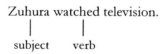

```
    Zuhura watched television.
      |          |
   subject     verb
```

    A modifier can come before or after the subject or the verb.

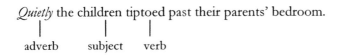

Quietly the children tiptoed past their parents' bedroom.

| | |
adverb   subject   verb

The children *quietly* tiptoed past their parents' bedroom.

| | |
subject   adverb   verb

The children tiptoed *quietly* past their parents' bedroom.

| | |
subject   verb   adverb

In questions, the word order varies from the normal simple sentence order.

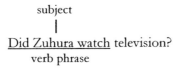

subject
|
Did Zuhura watch television?
verb phrase

2. A **compound sentence** consists of two statements or equal main clauses. These two statements are joined by coordinating conjunctions (see Chapter 46, Conjunctions).

    The two main clauses are connected by a coordinating conjunction. Each clause has its own subject and conjugated verb. Each, standing alone, could be a simple sentence.

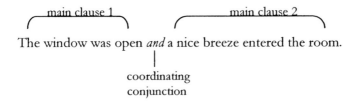

main clause 1   main clause 2

The window was open *and* a nice breeze entered the room.
|
coordinating
conjunction

3. A **complex sentence** is a sentence consisting of a main clause and one or more subordinate clauses.

The main clause in a complex sentence generally can stand alone as a complete sentence.

The subordinate clause cannot stand alone as a complete sentence; it depends on the main clause for its full meaning, and it is subordinate to the main clause.

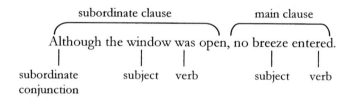

It makes sense to say "no breeze entered" without the first clause in the sentence; therefore, it is a main clause and could stand alone. It does not make sense to say "although the window was open" unless we add a conclusion; therefore, it is a subordinate clause.

It is important that you be able to distinguish a main clause from a subordinate clause. To do so will help you to write complex sentences and avoid sentence fragments. Subordinate clauses are introduced by subordinate conjunctions (see Chapter 46, Conjunctions) or relative pronouns (see Chapter 12).

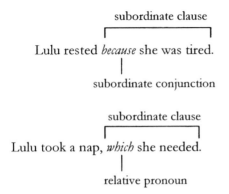

subordinate clause

Lulu rested *because* she was tired.

subordinate conjunction

subordinate clause

Lulu took a nap, *which* she needed.

relative pronoun

All relative clauses are adjectival since they modify nouns.

KWA KISWAHILI
Sentences are called **sentensi**.[20]   Phrases are called **virai**.
Clauses are called **vishazi**.   Sentences, phrases, and clauses
are generally identified the same way in Swahili as they are in
English.

SENTENSI
A sentence usually consists of at least of a subject (see
Chapter 19) and a verb (see Chapter 21).

> **Sudi alikimbia.**   *Sudi ran.*

---

[20] Other terms used for sentences include *mafungo ya maneno*
(singular: *fungo la maneno*) and **sentenso**. See G.W. Broomfield. *Sarufi
ya Kiswahili: A Grammar of Swahili in Swahili for Swahili-Speaking People*
(London: Sheldon Press, 1931).

However, because a Swahili verb contains the subject and the verb, a Swahili sentence may consist of only one word.

Alikimbia. *He ran.*

Depending on the verb, a sentence may also have direct and indirect objects (see Chapter 35 and 36).

In addition, a sentence may include various kinds of modifiers: adjectives (see Chapter 14), adverbs (see Chapter 45), prepositional phrases (see Chapter 47), and participial phrases (see Chapter 42). Modifiers are adjectival if they modify nouns. Modifiers are adverbial if they modify verbs, adjectives or adverbs.

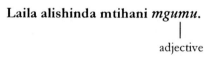

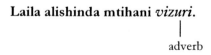

Laila alishinda mtihani <u>ingawa alikataa kusoma</u>.

adverbial prepositional phrase
telling how Laila passed

adjectival participial phrase modifying Laila

Laila, akijaribu sana kukumbuka kila kitu, alishinda mtihani.

It is important that you be able to recognize complete sentences and to distinguish phrases and clauses from complete sentences.

<u>VIRAI</u>

The various kinds of phrases are identified by the type of word beginning the phrase.

1. **kirai cha kihusishi** (*prepositional phrase*): a preposition + object of preposition

    karibu na **meza** (*near the table*)
    baada ya **pati** (*after the party*)
    mbele ya **gari** (*in front of the car*)

    A prepositional phrase is adjectival if it modifies a noun, adverbial if it modifies a verb. (See Chapter 47, Prepositions and Prepositional Phrases, and Chapter 48, Object of the Preposition.)

2. **kirai cha kitenzi cha -ki-** (*participial phrase*): starts with a participle

akiendesha gari *driving a car*

|

third person present active participle of **kuendesha**

akiendeshwa na hasira *driven by anger*

|

third person present passive participle of **kuendeshwa**

A participial phrase is adjectival since it modifies a noun. (See Chapter 42, Participles.)

3. **kirai cha kitenzijina** (*infinitive phrase*): starts with an infinitive

kusoma msamiati   *to study vocabulary*

| |

infinitive   object of **kusoma**

kumwagia mimea <u>kila siku</u>   *to water plants every day*

| |

infinitive   adverb modifying **kumwagia**

4. **kirai cha kitenzi** (*verb phrase*): a compound tense (see Chapter 43)

To recognize such phrases you need to recognize the auxiliary verb in a two word tense.

<u>VISHAZI</u>

There are two kinds of clauses: **main** (or **independent**) and **subordinate** (or **dependent**).

A main clause, called **kishazi kikuu** in Swahili, generally expresses a complete thought, the important idea of the sentence. If it stood alone with a capitalized first word and a period at the end, it could be a simple sentence.

A subordinate clause, called **kishazi tegemezi** in Swahili, cannot stand alone as a complete sentence. It must always be combined with a main clause.

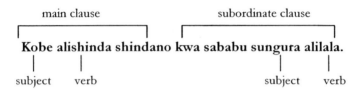

The turtle won the race because the rabbit slept.

A subordinate clause is adjectival if it modifes a noun, adverbial if it modifies a verb, adjective or adverb. Subordinate clauses are introduced by subordinate conjunctions, which are explained in more detail below.

TYPES OF *SENTENSI*
There are three types of sentences: **simple**, **compound**, and **complex**.

1. A simple sentence, called **sentensi sahili**, consists of only one main clause with no subordinate clauses. It has a subject and a conjugated verb. There may be many modifiers with a variety of word order.

    There is no set position for the verb in an Swahili sentence or cluause, but the subject always comes before the verb.

Zuhura aliangalia televisheni.

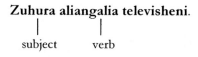

      subject   verb

Zuhura watched television.

A modifier can come after the verb.

Watoto walipita kimya chumba cha wazazi.

   subject   verb   adverb

The children passed their parents' room quietly.

In questions, the word order does not vary from the normal simple sentence order. The only difference between a sentence and a question is the addition of a question mark at the end, and, sometimes, the interrogative marker **Je** at the beginning.

> **Zuhura aliangalia televisheni?**
> or
> **Je, Zuhura aliangalia televisheni?**

2. A compound sentence, called **sentensi ambatani**, consists of two statements or equal main clauses. These two statements are joined by coordinating conjunctions (see Chapter 46, Conjunctions).

The two main clauses are connected by a coordinating conjunction. Each clause has its own subject and conjugated verb. Each, standing alone, could be a simple sentence.

The window was open and a nice wind entered the room.

3. A complex sentence, called **sentensi changamano**, is a sentence consisting of a main clause and one or more subordinate clauses.

The main clause in a complex sentence generally can stand alone as a complete sentence.

The subordinate clause cannot stand alone as a complete sentence; it depends on the main clause for its full meaning, and it is subordinate to the main clause.

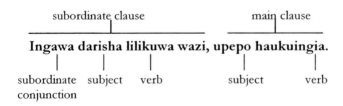

Although the window was open, the wind did not enter.

It makes sense to say "**upepo haukuingia**" without the first clause in the sentence; therefore, it is a main clause and could stand alone. It does not make sense to say "**ingawa dirisha lilikuwa wazi**" unless we add a conclusion; therefore, it is a subordinate clause.

It is important that you be able to distinguish a main clause from a subordinate clause. To do so will help you to write complex sentences and avoid sentence fragments. Subordinate clauses are introduced by subordinate conjunctions (see Chapter 46, Conjunctions) or relative constructions (see Chapter 12).

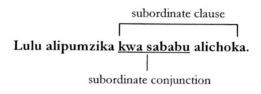

subordinate clause

Lulu alipumzika <u>kwa sababu</u> alichoka.

subordinate conjunction

Lulu rested because she was tired.

subordinate clause

Lulu alipata usingizi <u>ambao</u> alihitaji.

relative pronoun

Lulu got the sleep which she needed.

All relative constructions are adjectival since they modify nouns.

REVIEW

A. Circle whether the sentences below[21] are simple (S), compound (C) or complex (CX).

1. Swahili is a Bantu language and it is a member of the Niger-Congo family of African languages.

   S   C   CX

2. It developed as a lingua franca and trading language in most of East Africa, becoming the official language of Tanzania in 1967 and of Kenya in 1973.

   S   C   CX

3. It is also in use in parts of central and southern Africa.

   S   C   CX

4. It has a large body of literature, including poetry, novels, short stories, and theater.

   S   C   CX

---

[21] Adapted from "Swahili," *Oxford One-Volume Illustrated Encyclopedia* (London: Oxford, 1997).

B. Circle whether the following[22] are phrases (P), clauses (C), or sentences (S). All punctuation has been omitted.

1. Kenya's flag dates from 1963

                                                 P   C   S

2. when the country became independent

                                                 P   C   S

3. it is based on the flag of KANU (Kenya African National Unity)

                                               P   C   S

4. the political party that led the nationalist struggle

                                               P   C   S

5. the Masai warrior's shield and crossed spears represent the defense of freedom

                                               P   C   S

---

[22] Adapted from "Kenya," *Oxford One-Volume Illustrated Encylopedia* (London: Oxford, 1997).

Chapter 50
DECLARATIVE & INTERROGATIVE SENTENCES

A sentence is classified according to its purpose—whether it makes a statement or asks a question.

A **declarative sentence** is a sentence that makes a statement.

> *Zuhura owns many books.*

An **interrogative sentence** is a sentence that asks a question.

> *Does Zuhura own many books?*

In writing, an interrogative sentence has a question mark at the end. In speech, an interrogative question usually has a rising intonation.

IN ENGLISH

A declarative sentence can be changed to an interrogative sentence in one of three ways:

1. Add the auxiliary verb *do, does, did, will,* or *shall* before the subject and change the main verb to the dictionary form of the verb. *Do* and *does* are used to introduce a question in the present tense and *did* to introduce a question in the past tense (see Chapters 22-25 on the present and past tenses). *Will* or *shall* are used to introduce a question in the future tense (see Chapter 28, Future Tense).

- **present**   Sudi sits on the couch reading.
               Does Sudi sit on the couch reading?
- **past**   Sudi sat on the couch reading.
               Did Sudi sit on the couch reading?
- **future**   Sudi will sit on the couch reading.
               Will Sudi sit on the couch reading?

2. Some verbs allow you to change their word order, placing the verb before the subject.

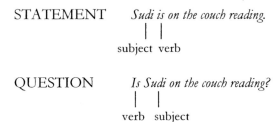

STATEMENT   *Sudi is on the couch reading.*
                  | |
                 subject verb

QUESTION   *Is Sudi on the couch reading?*
                  | |
                 verb   subject

3. Adding a short phrase at the end of the statement. This short phrase is sometimes called a **tag question**. A tag question is used when you expect a "yes" or "no" answer.

   Sudi isn't sitting on the couch, *is he?*
   Sudi is sitting on the couch, *isn't he?*

KWA KISWAHILI

Statements, called **matangazo**, can be changed into questions, called **maswali**, in one of three ways. Note that the word order does not change. In spoken Swahili, a rising intonation is used with questions, similar to the intonation used in English questions.

TANGAZO **Sudi amekaa kwenye kochi.**

1. Adding the question indicator **Je** to the beginning of the sentence and a question mark to the end. **Je** is usually used with questions that expect a "yes" or "no" answer.

SWALI **Je, Sudi amekaa kwenye kochi?**

2. Adding a question mark to the end of the sentence, when expecting a "yes" or "no" answer.

SWALI **Sudi amekaa kwenye kochi?**

3. Adding a tag question, called **kirai shawishi**, to the end of the sentence. **Sivyo** is the most common tag question. It expects a "yes" answer, but a "no" answer may be given.

SWALI **Sudi amekaa kwenye kochi, sivyo?**
SWALI **Sudi amekaa kwenye kochi, au sivyo?**

TAKE NOTE

All three of these methods are used for questions that expect a "yes" or "no" answer. Questions that expect a more complicated answer usually use interrogative pronouns or adjectives (see Chapters 9 and 17).

REVIEW

Change the following sentences[23] to questions.

1. *The Republic of Kenya straddles the Equator in East Africa.*

---

2. *Mombasa lies on the narrow coastal plane.*

---

3. *Most of Kenya comprises high scrubland around Lake Turkana.*

---

4. *In the southwest are the Kenyan highlands.*

---

5. *Mount Kenya is the country's highest peak.*

---

[23] English sentences adapted from "Kenya," *Oxford One-Volume Illustrated Encyclopedia* (London: Oxford, 1997).

6. Nairobi is the capital.

---

7. The Great Rift Valley cuts through western Kenya.

---

8. Mombasa is hot and humid.

---

9. The coast is lined with mangrove swamps.

---

10. Kenya is the world's fourth largest tea producer.

---

11. Kiswahili kinasemwa Tanzania.

---

12. Watu wengi wanasema Kiswahili kama lugha ya pili.

---

13. Waswahili wanakaa pwani ya Afrika ya Mashariki.

---

14. Wanafunzi wengi wa Kimarekani wanachagua kusoma Kiswahili.

Chapter 51
CONDITIONAL SENTENCES

Sentences that state that if a certain condition exists then a certain result can be expected are called **conditional sentences**. They are complex sentences (see Chapter 49, Sentences, Phrases and Clauses) consisting of two parts.

1. a **condition**, the subordinate clause, which is introduced by *if* or *unless*
2. a **conclusion**, the main clause, which is the result of the condition

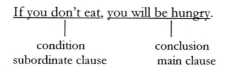

        If you don't eat, you will be hungry.
              | |
          condition   conclusion
      subordinate clause   main clause

IN ENGLISH

There are three types of conditional sentences.

1. simple conditions

The condition can take place in the present, past or future.

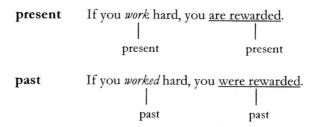

present   If you *work* hard, you are rewarded.
                      | |
                   present   present

past   If you *worked* hard, you were rewarded.
                       | |
                     past   past

future   If you *work* hard, you <u>will be rewarded</u>.

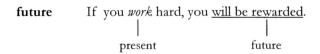

                    present   future

- Although the present tense is used, a future time
  is implied.

1. **"should-would" conditions**
                    Some doubt is implied about the
                    possibility of the condition occurring, as
                    expressed by the "should" in the
                    condition and "would" in the conclusion.

If you *should* work hard, you *would* be rewarded.

2. **contrary-to-fact conditions**
                    There is no possibility of the condition
                    actually occurring; as the name implies,
                    the condition is contrary-to-fact. These
                    statements can only be made about the
                    present or past.

present	If you <u>were working</u> hard, you would be rewarded. subjunctive • Implication: You are not working hard. *Were* is an example of one of the rare uses of the subjunctive in English. See Chapter 39, *The Subjunctive Mood.*
past	If you <u>had worked</u>, you would have been rewarded. past perfect indicative • Implication: You did not work hard.

KWA KISWAHILI

The same three types of conditional sentences exist, but two different constructions are used.

1. **sharti sahili** (*simple conditions*)

The condition can take place in the present, past or future.

present	**Kama ukifanya kazi, unapewa tuzo.**
	present participle[24] present
	If you work you will be rewarded.
past	**Kama ulifanya kazi, ulipewa tuzo**
	past past
	If you worked, you were rewarded.
future	**Kama ukifanya kazi, utapewa tuzo.**
	present participle future
	If you work, you will be rewarded
	• Although the present participle is used, a future time is implied.

1. **hali ya sharti** (*the conditional mood*)

The conditional mood is used to express both should-would and contrary-to-fact conditions.

---

[24] Note that the present participle can be used to imply *if* with or without the word **kama** (*if*): **Ukifanya kazi, utapewa thawabu.** See Chapter 42, Participles.

Kama u*ng*efanya kazi, u*ng*epewa tuzo.
If you should work, you would be rewarded. (should-would)
or
If you were working you would be rewarded. (contrary-to-fact)

Kama u*ng*eli*fanya kazi, u*ng*eli*pewa tuzo.
If you had worked, you would have been rewarded.

REVIEW

Circle whether the conditional sentences below[25] are simple (S), should-would (SW) or contrary-to-fact (CF).

1. *If you visit Uganda, you will see many lakes and swamps.*
                                    S   SW   CF

2. *If you should travel toward the west, you would see an arm of the Great Rift Valley.*

                                    S   SW   CF

3. *If the Ugandan flag used green instead of yellow, it would have the same colors as the Kenyan flag.*

                                    S   SW   CF

4. *If the National Resistance Army had not captured Kampala in 1986, Museveni would not have become president.*
                                    S   SW   CF

---

[25] Adapted from "Uganda," *Oxford One-Volume Illustrated Encyclopedia* (London: Oxford, 1997).

5. *If you travel east from Kampala, you cross Lake Victoria and enter Tanzania.*

S   SW   CF

6. **Kama ungeliniuliza, ungelijua kwamba pati ni leo.**

S   SW   CF

7. **Kama ukitaka kuja, niambie tu.**

S   SW   CF

8. **Tutafurahi sana kama ukija na wenzako.**

S   SW   CF

9. **Ungeweza kuleta chakula kidogo?**

S   SW   CF

10. **Kama huwezi, si kitu.**

S   SW   CF

Chapter 52
DIRECT & INDIRECT STATEMENTS

A **direct statement** is the transmission of a message by direct quotation. The message is set in quotation marks.

> *My mother said, "I like your friend Laila."*

An **indirect statement** is the reporting of a message without quoting the words directly. It does not use quotation marks.

> *My mother said (that) she likes my friend Laila.*

Notice in the first sentence above that the speaker's first person pronoun (*I like* . . .) in the direct statement changes to the third person pronoun (*she likes*) to agree logically with the perspective of the person doing the reporting. Also, in the second sentence, the possessive adjective *your* has changed to *my*.

IN ENGLISH

An indirect statement is easy to recognize since the reported message is introduced by *that* forming a subordinate clause (see Chapter 49, Sentences, Phrases and Clauses) used as an object of the verb. No quotation marks are used. Frequently, especially in speech, the introductory word *that* is omitted.

> *The teacher said (that) we should study tonight.*
> *The president claims (that) he will lower taxes.*

When the direct statement is transformed into a reported message, there is usually a shift in tense to maintain the logical time sequence in indirect statement.

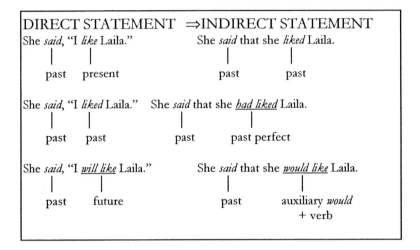

DIRECT STATEMENT ⇒INDIRECT STATEMENT

She *said,* "I *like* Laila."   She *said* that she *liked* Laila.

| | | |
past present   past   past

She *said,* "I *liked* Laila." She *said* that she *had liked* Laila.

| | | |
past past   past   past perfect

She *said,* "I *will like* Laila."   She *said* that she *would like* Laila.

| | | |
past future   past   auxiliary *would*
                                   + verb

KWA KISWAHILI

Indirect statements, called **kauli zilizotajwa,** are used not only after verbs of saying, but also after verbs of thinking, feeling, sensing, writing and the like. Swahili uses the introductory words **kwamba** or **kuwa** like the *that* of the English construction. Indirect statement is very commonly used in Swahili, but follows rules slightly different from those used in English. Note that there is not usually a shift in tenses when a direct statement is transformed into an indirect statement.

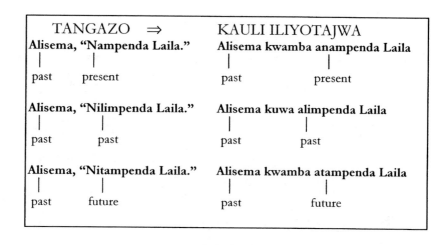

REVIEW

Change the direct statements below to indirect statements.

1. Salim told me, "My ankle really hurts today."

---

2. I thought, "Of course it does; you fall down all the time."

---

3. "Maybe you should go to the doctor," I said.

---

4. "Alright," said Salim. "I'll go."

---

5. Salim went to the doctor, who told him, "You have a sprained ankle."

---

6. Salim aliniambia, "Mguu wangu unaumia leo."

---

7. Nilifikiri, "Bila shaka. Unaanguka mara kwa mara."

---

8. "Labda itabidi uende kwa daktari," nilisema.

---

9. "Sawa," Salim alisema. "Nitaenda."

---

10. Salim alienda kwa daktari ambaye alimwambia, "Ulivunja mguu wako."

Chapter 53
COMPARISONS

When adjectives are used to compare the qualities of the nouns they modify, or when adverbs are used to compare the qualities of the verbs they modify, they change forms. This change is called **comparison.**

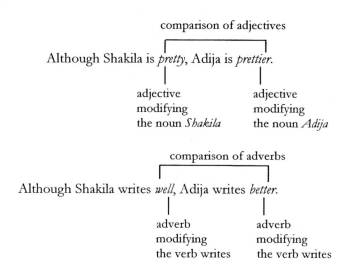

comparison of adjectives

Although Shakila is *pretty*, Adija is *prettier*.

adjective modifying the noun *Shakila*

adjective modifying the noun *Adija*

comparison of adverbs

Although Shakila writes *well*, Adija writes *better*.

adverb modifying the verb writes

adverb modifying the verb writes

IN ENGLISH
There are three degrees of comparison and each degree is formed in a different way.

1. The **positive form** refers to the quality of a person or thing. It is simply the adjective or adverb form.

    Usi is *short*.   Juma runs *fast*.
    The fabric is *colorful*.
    The presidents speaks *quickly*.

2. The **comparative form** compares the quality of one person, thing or action with that of another person, thing or action. It is formed:

- by adding *-er* to short adjectives and to adverbs that do not end in *-ly*.

  Usi is *shorter* than Mwanampate.
  Juma runs *faster* than other boys his age.

- by placing *more* or *less* in front of longer adjectives and most adverbs.

  This fabric is *less colorful* than that fabric.
  This president speaks *more quickly* than the last one.

1. The **superlative form** is used to stress the highest or lowest degree of a quality. It is formed:

   - by adding *-est* to short adjectives and to adverbs that do not end in *-ly*.

     Usi is the *shortest* teacher in the room.
     Of all the boys, Juma runs *fastest*.

- by placing *most, least, very* or *exceedingly* in front of longer adjectives and most adverbs.

  This fabric is the *most colorful* one I have ever seen.
  This president speaks *very quickly.*

Some of the most common adjectives and adverbs have irregular comparative and superlative forms; here are a few examples.

bad, ill	*worse*	*worst*
far	*farther (distance)*	*farthest*
further (additional)	*furthest*	
good, well	*better*	*best*
little	*less, lesser*	*least*
littler	*least*	
much, many	*more*	*most*

KWA KISWAHILI

Comparison is called **ulinganishaji**, from the verb **kulinganisha** , *to compare.* Swahili has the same three degrees of comparison that exist in English, but they are expressed differently.

1. The positive form, called **umbo halisi**, is simply the adjective or adverb. See Chapter 14, Adjectives, and Chapter 45, Adverbs.

   Usi ni *mfupi*.
   Usi is short.
   Juma anakimbia *kwa haraka*.
   Juma runs quickly.

2. The comparative form, called **umbo linganishi**, compares the quality of one person, thing or action with

that of another person thing or action. It is formed by
using a comparative preposition after the adjective or
adverb compared. These conjunctions include **kuliko,
zaidi ya, kupita,** and **kushinda.**

> **Usi ni mfupi <u>kuliko</u> Mwanampate.**
> (*Usi is shorter <u>than</u> Mwanampate.*)
> **Juma anakimbia kwa haraka <u>zaida ya</u> wavulana
> wengine.**
> (*Juma runs faster <u>than</u> other boys.*)
> **Kitambaa hiki kina rangi chache <u>kupita</u> kile.**
> (*This fabric has fewer colors <u>than</u> that one.*)
> **Rais huyu anasema upesi <u>kuwashinda</u> wengine.**
> (This president speaks more quickly <u>than</u> others.)

When the object of comparison is not specified, the
adjective **zaidi** (*more*) is used without any conjunction.

> **Mtu huyu ni mwema zaidi.**
> *This person is better.*
> **Nina vitabu vyingi zaidi.**
> *I have more books.*

3. The superlative form, called **umbo lenye sifa ya juu (au ya chini) kabisa**, is formed by using the comparative prepositions described above, followed by the noun or adjective **-ote** *(all)*. The dash (-) indicates that **-ote** must agree in class with the plural noun to which it refers.

> **Usi ni mwalimu mfupi <u>kuliko wote</u>.**
> *(Usi is the shortest teacher.)*
> Literally: *Usi is a short teacher <u>than all (the others)</u>.*

> **Juma anakimbia kwa haraka zaida ya wavulana wote.**
> *(Juma runs fastest of all the boys.)*
> Literally: *Juma runs with speed greater than all the boys.*

> **Kitambaa hiki kina rangi nyingi <u>kupita vyote</u>.**
> *(This fabric is the most colorful of all.)*
> Literally: *This fabric has many colors <u>to surpass all</u>.*

> **Rais huyu anasema upesi <u>kuwashinda wote</u>.**
> *This president speaks the most quickly.*
> Literally: *This presidents speaks quickly <u>to conquer all</u>.*

TAKE NOTE

Because they are also verbs, the Swahili comparative prepositions *kupita*, which literally means *to pass or surpass,* and **kushinda**, which literally means *to conquer*, must take object markers when followed by nouns that refer to people. See Chapter 35, Direct Objects.

REVIEW

In the sentences[26] below, draw an arrow from the adjective to the noun it modifies. Circle the degree of comparison: positive (P), comparative (C) or superlative (S).

1. *His travel expenses were greater than mine.*

                                    P   C   S

2. *Juma and Adija's wedding was very traditional.*

                                    P   C   S

3. *My cousin is the best swimmer in town.*

                                    P   C   S

4. *The novelist is respected.*

                                    P   C   S

5. *Hud is the least competitive boy on the team.*

                                    P   C   S

---

[26] Sentences 6-10 are adapted from G.W. Broomfield, *Sarufi ya Kiswahili* (London: Sheldon Press, 1931).

6. Huyu ni bwana mkubwa.

                                    P   C   S

7. Hawa ni watu wema kuliko wengine.

                                    P   C   S

8. Ng'ombe ni mrefu kuliko kondoo.

                                    P   C   S

9. Amepata fedha nyingi zaidi ya ndugu yake.

                                    P   C   S

10. Amekuwa hodari lakini sasa ni hodari zaidi.

                                    P   C   S

MISC.

Chapter 54
REDUPLICATION

Reduplication is a process of creating new words by doubling a word or part of word. For example:

hoity-toity

IN ENGLISH
Reduplication is not common in English, but it does occur. Here are some examples:

higglety-pigglety
hocus-pocus

KWA KISWAHILI
Reduplication is called **urudufu**, from the adjective **rudufu**, which means *double or twofold* and the verb **kurudufu**, which means *to double*. Reduplication in Swahili is used to form new words or to exaggerate a word's original meaning. Note that the part of speech can also be modified, and that reduplicated words comprise various parts of speech.

REDUPLICATED VERBS = **VITENZI RUDUFU**

> **kuenda** (verb) *to go*
> ⇒ **kuendaenda** (verb) *to go on and on*

REDUPLICATED NOUNS = **MAJINA RUDUFU**

> **kupinda** (verb) *to bend, twist, fold, bend up*
>> ⇒ **kipindupindu** (noun) *seizure, convulsions, cholera*

> **kuvunja** (verb) *to break, to break down, to break up*
>> ⇒ **kivunjavunja** (noun) *praying mantis* (from a superstition that should you happen to kill one, you will break the next thing you touch)[27]

REDUPLICATED ADVERBS = **VIELEZI RUDUFU**

> **sana** (adverb) *very*
>> ⇒ **sana sana** (adverb) *extremely*

> **sawa** (adjective) *like, alike, equal, the same, just, right, level*
>> ⇒ **sawasawa** (adverb) *equally, just the same*

Another use of reduplication is to form intensive pronouns, called **viwakilishi vya nguvu**, or reduplicated demonstratives, **vionyeshi rudufu,** from the demonstrative adjective/pronoun **-le**. See Chapter 18, Demonstrative Adjectives and Chapter 10, Demonstrative Pronouns.

---

[27] Frederick Johnson. *A Standard Swahili-English Dictionary.* 1939. Nairobi & Dar es Salaam: Oxford University Press, 1999.

Nataka kitabu <u>kile kile</u>.
I want <u>that same</u> book (as the one mentioned previously).

Alihudhuria shule <u>ile ile</u>.
He attended <u>that same</u> school (as the one mentioned previously).

TAKE NOTE

Not all words can be reduplicated and still signify anything meaningful. You should be able to recognize and guess at the meaning of reduplicated words, but be cautious about forming them yourself.

Chapter 55
INTERJECTIONS

An **interjection** or **exclamation** is a cry, an expression of strong feeling or emotion. It usually occurs at the beginning of a sentence, and stands apart from the grammar of the sentence. For example:

> *Hey!* Where have you been?
>
> interjection

IN ENGLISH

There is a great variety of such emotional words, including most words of swearing and profanity. They belong to both written and spoken language, but are separated from the main clause by a comma; the sentence usually ends with an exclamation mark.

> *Ah,* the water feels great.
> *Yikes,* what in the the world are you doing?!

KWA KISWAHILI

Interjections are called **vihusishi**, from the verb **kuhisi**, *to feel*. A variety of emotional words exists in Swahili, including expressions of awe, anger, fear, joy, sadness and the evoking of God. An interjection is invariable; it never changes form. Here are a few examples.

INTERJECTION	EMOTION/PURPOSE EXPRESSED
Lo!	*surprise*
Ah!	*grief*
Ole!	*grief*
Ee-e-e-e	*consolation*
Haya!	*agreement/attention-getting*
Ala!	*annoyance, impatience*
Inshallah	*if God is willing (from Arabic)*

GLOSSARY

A

active verb(s) *kitenzi cha
(vitenzi vya) kufanya*
7/8
adjective(s) *kivumishi
(vivumishi)* 7/8
adopted word *neno
lililohotolewa (maneno
yaliyohotolewa)* 5/6
adverb(s) *kielezi (vielezi)* 7/8
affirmative sentence(s)
*sentensi ya kukubali
(sentensi za kukubali)*
7/8
agglutination *uambishaji 14*
applied extension(s)
*mnyambuliko wa
(minyambuliko ya)
kufanyia 3/4*
article(s) *kibainishi (vibainishi)*
7/8
attributive adjective(s)
*kivumishi angama
(vivumishi angama)
7/8*
auxiliary verb(s) *kitenzi
kisaidizi (vitenzi
visaidizi)* 7/8

C

causative extension(s)
*mnyambuliko wa
(minyambuliko ya)
kufanyiza 3/4*
class(es) *ngeli 9/10*
clause(s) *kishazi (vishazi)* 7/8
command(s) *amri 9/10*
common noun(s) *nomino ya
(za) jumla 9/10;
nomino ya (za) jamii
9/10*
comparison(s) *ulinganishaji
14*
conditional sentence(s)
sentensi sharti 9/10
conjunction(s) *kiunganishi
(viunganishi)* 7/8

D

declarative sentence(s)
tangazo 9/10
demonstrative adjective(s)
*kionyeshi (vionyeshi)
7/8*
demonstrative pronoun(s)
*kionyeshi (vionyeshi)
7/8*
direct object(s) *shamirisho
yambwa 9/10*
direct statement(s) *kauli
halisi* **9/10**

F

function(s) *kazi* 9/10
future tense *wakati ujao* 11

G

gerund(s) *kitenzijina*
  (vitenzijina) 7/8

H

habitual present tense
wakati uliopo wa kawaida 11

I

imperative(s) *amri* 9/10
imperfect tense *tensi*
  isiyotimilifu 9
indefinite pronoun(s)
  kiwakilishi kisicho
  (viwakilishi visivyo)
  dhahiri 7/8
indirect object(s) *shamirisho*
  yambiwa 10
indirect statement(s) *kauli*
  iliyotajwa (zilizotajwa)
  9/10

infinitive(s) *kitenzijina*
  (vitenzijina) 7/8
infixed relative(s) *kirejeshi-*
  kati (virejeshi-kati) 7/8
interjection(s) *kihisishi*
  (vihisishi) 7/8
intensive pronoun(s)
  kiwakilishi cha
  (viwakilishi vya) nguvu
interrogative adjective(s)
  kivumishi cha
  (vivumishi vya) kuuliza
  7/8
interrogative pronoun(s)
  kiwakilishi cha
  (viwakilishi vya)
  kuuliza 7/8
intransitive verb(s) *kitenzi*
  kisoelekezi (vitenzi
  visoelekezi) 7/8

L

locative(s) *jina la mahali*
  (majina ya mahali) 5/6

M

meaning(s) *maana* 9/10
mood(s) *hali* 9/10

N

nominal prefix *kiambishi awali cha jina (viambishi awali vya majina) 5/6*

noun(s) *(ma)jina 5/6; nomino 9/10*

number *namba ya jina 9*

O

object infix(es) *kiambishi (viambishi) kati cha (vya) shamirisho* **9/10**

object(s) *mtendwa (watendwa) 1/2; shamirisho 9/10*

P

part(s) of speech *aina ya neno (aina za maneno) 5/6*

passive extension(s) *mnyambuliko wa (minyambuliko ya) kufanywa 3/4*

passive verb(s) *kitenzi cha (vitenzi vya) kufanywa 7/8*

past tense *wakati uliopita 11*

perfect tense *tensi timilifu 9*

phrase(s) *kirai (virai) 7/8*

possessive adjective(s) *kimilikishi (vimilikishi) 7/8*

possessive contraction(s) *kifupisho cha kimilikishi (vifupisho vya vimilikishi) 7/8*

possessive pronoun(s) *kimilikishi (vimilikishi) 7/8*

predicate adjective(s) *kivumishi arifu (vivumishi arifa) 7/8; kivumishi cha maelezo (vivumishi vya maelezo) 7/8*

preposition(s) *kihusishi (vihusishi) 7/8*

prepositional clause(s) *kishazi cha kihusishi (vishazi vya vihusishi) 7/8*

present tense *wakati uliopo 11*

present continuous tense *wakati uliopo unaoendelea 11*

pronoun(s) *kiwakilishi (viwakilishi) nomino 7/8*

proper noun *nomino kamili 9/10; nomino ya (za) pekee 9/10*

R

reduplicated demonstrative(s) *kionyeshi (vionyeshi) rudufu* 7/8
reduplication *urudufu* 14
relative construction(s) *kirejeshi (***virejeshi***)* 7/8
reversive extension(s) *mnyambuliko wa (minyambuliko ya) kufanyua* 3/4

S

sentences *sentensi*
simple present tense *wakati uliopo sahili* 11
stative extension(s) *mnyambuliko wa (minyambuliko ya) kufanyika* 3/4
subject prefix(es) *kiambishi awali (viambishi awali)* 7/8
subject(s) *mtenda (watenda) 3/4; kiima (viima)* 7/8
subjunctive(s) *dhamira tegemezi* 9/10
synopsis *muhtasari 3; ufupisho 14; kidokezo 7*

T

tag question(s) *kirai shawishi (virai shawishi)* 7/8
tenseless relative(s) *kirejeshi (virejeshi) bila tensi* 7/8
reflexive infix *kiambishi kati cha kujirejea* 7
transitive verb(s) *kitenzi elekezi (vitenzi elekezi)* 7/8
two-word tense(s) *tensi ya (za) maneno mawili*

V

verbal noun(s) *kitenzijina (vitenzijina)* 7/8
verb extension(s) *mnyambuliko (minyambuliko)*
verb tense(s) *tensi 9/10; wakati (nyakati)* 11/10
verb(s) *kitenzi (vitenzi)* 7/8

KISWAHILI KWA KIINGEREZA

A

aina ya neno *part of speech*
aina za maneno *parts of speech*
amri *imperative(s)*

D

dhamira tegemezi *subjunctive(s)*

H

hali *mood(s)*

J

jina *noun*
jina la mahali *locative*

K

kauli halisi *direct statements*
kauli iliyotajwa *indirect statement*
kauli zilizotajwa *indirect statements*
kazi *functions*
kiambishi awali *subject prefix*
kiambishi awali cha jina *nominal prefix*
kiambishi kati cha kujirejea *reflexive infix*
kiambishi kati cha shamirisho *object infix*
kibainishi *article*
kidokezo *synopsis*
kielezi *adverb*
kihisishi *interjection*
kihusishi *preposition*
kiima *subject*
kimilikishi *possessive pronoun*
kionyeshi *demonstrative adjective; demonstrative pronoun*
kionyeshi rudufu *reduplicated demonstrative*
kirai *phrase*
kirai shawishi *tag question*
kirejeshi *relative construction*
kirejeshi bila tensi *tenseless relative*
kirejeshi-kati *infixed relative*
kishazi *clause*

kishazi cha kihusishi
  prepositional clause
kitenzi *verb*
kitenzi cha kufanya *active*
  verb
kitenzi cha kufanywa
  passive verb
kitenzi elekezi *transitive verb*
kitenzi kisaidizi *auxiliary*
  verb
kitenzi kisoelekezi
  intransitive verb
kitenzijina *infinitive; verbal*
  noun; gerund
kiunganishi *conjunction*
kivumishi *adjective*
kivumishi angama
  attributive adjective
kivumishi arifa *predicate*
  adjective
kivumishi cha kuuliza
  interrogative adjective
kivumishi cha maelezo
  predicate adjective
kiwakilishi cha nguvu
  intensive pronoun
kiwakilishi nomino *pronoun*
kiwakilishi cha kuuliza
  interrogative pronoun
kiwakilishi kisicho dhahiri
  indefinite pronoun

M

maana *meaning*
majina *nouns*
majina ya mahali *locatives*

matangazo *declarative sentences*
minyambuliko ya kufanyia
  applied extensions
minyambuliko ya
  kufanyika *stative*
  extensions
minyambuliko ya
  kufanyiza *causative*
  extensions
minyambuliko ya
  kufanyua *reversive*
  extensions
minyambuliko ya
  kufanywa *passive*
  extensions
minyambuliko *verb extensions*
mnyambuliko *verb extension*
mnyambuliko wa kufanyia
  applied extension
mnyambuliko wa
  kufanyika *stative*
  extension
mnyambuliko wa
  kufanyiza *causative*
  extension
mnyambuliko wa
  kufanyua *reversive*
  extension
mnyambuliko wa
  kufanywa *passive*
  extension
mtenda *subject*
mtendwa *object*
muhtasari *synopsis, summary*

N

namba ya jina *number*
ngeli *class(es)*
nomino *noun(s)*
nomino ambatani *compound noun(s)*
nomino kamili *proper noun(s)*
nomino ya jamii *common noun*
nomino ya jumla *collective noun*
nomino ya pekee *proper noun*
nomino za jamii *common nouns*
nomino za jumla *collective nouns*
nomino za pekee *proper nouns*
nyakati *verb tenses*

S

sentensi *sentence(s)*
sentensi sharti *conditional sentence(s)*
sentensi ya kanusho *negative sentence*
sentensi ya kukubali *affirmative sentence*
sentensi za kanusho *negative sentences*
sentensi za kukubali *affirmative sentences*
shamirisho *object(s)*

shamirisho yambiwa *indirect object(s)*
shamirisho yambwa *direct object(s)*

T

tangazo *declarative sentence*
tensi *verb tense(s)*
tensi isiyotimilifu *imperfect tense*
tensi timilifu *perfect tense*
tensi ya maneno mawili *two-word tense*
tensi za maneno mawili *two-word tenses*

U

uambishaji *agglutination*
ufupisho *synopsis*
ulinganishaji *comparison(s)*
urudufu *reduplication*

V

viambishi awali *subject prefixes*
viambishi awali vya majina *nominal prefixes*
viambishi vya shamirisho *object infixes*
vibainishi *articles*

vielezi *adverbs*
vihisishi *interjections*
vihusishi *prepositions*
viima *subjects*
vimilikishi *possessive pronouns*
vionyeshi *demonstrative adjectives; demonstrative pronouns*
vionyeshi rudufu *reduplicated demonstratives*
virai *phrases*
virai shawishi *tag questions*
virejeshi *relative constructions*
virejeshi bila tensi *tenseless relatives*
virejeshi-kati *infixed relatives*
vishazi *clauses*
vishazi vya vihusishi *prepositional clauses*
vitenzi *verbs*
vitenzi vya kufanya *active verbs*
vitenzi vya kufanywa *passive verbs*
vitenzi elekezi *transitive verbs*
vitenzi visaidizi *auxiliary verbs*
vitenzi visoelekezi *intransitive verbs*
vitenzijina *infinitives; verbal nouns; gerunds*
viunganishi *conjunctions*
vivumishi *adjectives*
vivumishi angama *attributive adjectives*
vivumishi arifa *predicate adjectives*
vivumishi vya kuuliza *interrogative adjectives*

vivumishi vya maelezo *predicate adjectives*
viwakilishi vya nguvu *intensive pronouns*
viwakilishi nomino *pronouns*
viwakilishi vya kuuliza *interrogative pronouns*
viwakilishi visivyo dhahiri *indefinite pronouns*

W

wakati *verb tense*
wakati ujao *future tense*
wakati uliopita *past tense*
wakati uliopo *present tense*
wakati uliopo *simple present tense*
wakati uliopo unaoendelea *present continuous tense*
wakati uliopo wa kawaida *habitual present tense*
watenda *subjects*
watendwa *objects*

INDEX

A

-a- tense, 2, 98, 149, 169, 170, 178

active verbs, 3, 303, 304, 419, 426, 430

adjectives, v, 1, 2, 5, 13, 14, 16, 26, 27, 30, 33, 34, 36, 37, 38, 47, 50, 51, 76, 77, 78, 79, 82, 87, 90, 91, 92, 105, 106, 107, 108, 113, 114, 115, 116, 117, 118, 119, 121, 122, 123, 124, 125, 126, 127, 128, 131, 132, 133, 134, 135, 136, 141, 143, 282, 289, 290, 291, 292, 293, 311, 312, 313, 314, 315, 330, 342, 343, 349, 352, 362, 371, 375, 376, 377, 378, 379, 380, 385, 386, 419, 420, 421, 422, 426, 427, 430

adopted words, 38, 39, 419

adverbs, 3, 5, 13, 184, 311, 312, 313, 314, 315, 330, 342, 343, 344, 346, 349, 351, 352, 353, 375, 376, 377, 378, 386, 419, 426, 429

agglutination, 2, 164, 419, 429

agreement, 8, 96, 116, 123, 390

aina ya neno, see *part of speech*, 422, 425

applied extension, 256, 419, 427

articles, 1, 13, 25, 26, 27, 142, 419, 426, 429

auxiliary verbs, 2, 177, 181, 183, 237, 238, 242, 296, 297, 299, 304, 344, 351, 359, 419, 426, 430

C

causative extension, 3, 277, 282, 283, 419, 427

class, 1, 8, 9, 16, 29, 30, 31, 32, 33, 34, 35, 36, 37, 38, 39, 40, 41, 42, 43, 44, 48, 61, 74, 75, 76, 82, 83, 84, 85, 86, 87, 91, 96, 97, 98, 99, 106, 109, 116, 117, 118, 123, 125, 128, 132, 133, 136, 137, 138, 139, 140, 141, 147, 149, 150, 151, 152, 153, 154, 155, 156, 157, 169, 170, 171, 192, 196, 205, 211, 212, 213, 214, 215, 221, 222, 230, 231, 232, 233, 234, 244, 245, 246, 248, 253, 270, 271, 281, 283, 289, 290, 312, 313, 314, 320, 321, 324, 332, 379, 419, 428, 422, 424, 425

clauses, 4, 61, 93, 94, 95, 96, 100, 101, 102, 107, 122, 125, 268, 270, 319, 320, 322, 323, 341, 343, 345, 346, 347, 348, 350, 351, 352, 353, 354, 355, 357, 365, 371, 389, 419, 422, 426, 430

collective nouns, 32, 41, 42, 428

commands, 260, 263, 264, 265, 270, 271, 272, 419

common nouns, 20, 22, 34, 419, 428

comparisons, 4, 330, 375, 377, 378, 380, 419, 429

compound tenses, 3, 181, 183, 242, 295, 296, 298, 299, 301, 351

conditional sentences, 4, 365, 367, 368, 419, 428

conjunctions, 3, 13, 184, 319, 320, 322, 323, 324, 346, 347, 348, 352, 353, 354, 355, 378, 419, 426, 430

D

declarative sentences, 359, 420, 427, 429

demonstratives, 26, 27, 65, 81, 82, 83, 84, 85, 86, 87, 114, 135, 136, 137, 138, 139, 140, 141, 142, 143, 386, 420, 423, 426, 430

dhamira tegemezi, see *subjunctive*, 261, 269, 423, 425

direct objects, 3, 15, 47, 49, 50, 60, 64, 67, 71, 72, 73, 74, 75, 76, 95, 100, 101, 162, 243, 244, 247, 249, 250, 251, 252, 253, 255, 277, 278, 282, 303, 306, 331, 336, 337, 342, 349, 420, 429

direct statement, 371, 372, 373, 420, 426

F

function, 1, 13, 15, 16, 23, 26, 48, 50, 54, 59, 61, 63, 64, 67, 68, 71, 76, 94, 98, 99, 145, 146, 147, 237, 242, 247, 252, 253, 289, 290, 291, 299, 312, 330, 337, 420, 426

future perfect tense, 297, 300

future tense, 7, 98, 99, 199, 200, 203, 205, 207, 210, 211, 214, 215, 217, 225, 228, 229, 233, 234, 235, 239, 259, 261, 297, 299, 300, 359, 420, 430

G

gender, 23, 105
gerundives, 47, 289, 290, 292
gerunds, 40, 45, 46, 47, 48, 51, 53, 54, 168, 292, 420, 426, 430

I

imperfect tense, 321, 421, 429
indefinite pronouns, 1, 61, 105, 106, 421, 427, 430
indicative mood, 3, 259, 261, 320
indirect objects, 3, 60, 67, 68, 71, 72, 73, 74, 75, 76, 77, 243, 244, 251, 252, 253, 255, 257, 331, 335, 337, 342, 349, 421, 429
indirect statement, 4, 371, 372, 373, 421, 426
infinitive, 46
infinitives, 1, 40, 45, 46, 48, 51, 53, 54, 153, 170, 171, 172, 173, 175, 184, 192, 200, 229, 332, 344, 351, 421, 426, 430
infixed relative, 1, 98, 421, 426, 430

intensive pronouns, 386, 421, 427, 430
interjections, 4, 13, 389, 421, 426, 429
interrogative adjectives, 2, 77, 78, 79, 114, 131, 132, 133, 134, 421, 427, 430
interrogative pronouns, 1, 60, 71, 73, 74, 77, 78, 79, 133, 362, 421, 427, 430
intransitive verbs, 2, 162, 163, 249, 421, 426, 430

J

jina, see *noun*, 21, 32, 33, 97, 116, 123, 124, 137, 138, 140, 141, 421, 422, 425, 426, 428

K

-ka- tense, 183, 184
kauli zilizotajwa, see *indirect statements*, 372, 426
kazi see *function*, 38, 39, 50, 367, 368, 420, 426
kiambishi awali cha jina, see *nominal prefix*, 33, 422, 426

kiambishi awali, see
subject prefix, 33, 149,
422, 423, 426

**kiambishi kati cha
shamirisho**, see *object
infix*, 244, 426

kimilikishi, see *possessive
pronoun*, 90, 123, 125,
422, 426

kionyeshi, see
demonstrative, 81, 136,
420, 423, 426

kirejeshi bila tensi, see
tenseless relative, 99, 426

kirejeshi-kati, see *infixed
relative*, 98, 421, 426

kishazi, see *clause*, 351,
352, 419, 422, 426

kitenzi cha kufanya, see
active verb, 304, 426

kitenzi, see *verb*, 277, 290,
304, 350, 351, 419, 421,
422, 423, 424, 426

kitenzijina, see *verbal noun*,
48, 351, 420, 421, 424,
426

kivumishi angama, see
attributive adjective, 117,
419, 426

kivumishi cha maelezo,
see *predicate adjective*, 117,
422, 427

L

linking verbs, 115, 117

locative suffixes, 40, 41,
220, 221, 223

locatives, 2, 40, 41, 220,
221, 222, 223, 332, 421,
425, 427

M

majina ya mahali, see
locatives, 40, 421, 427

majina, see *nouns*, 21, 30,
40, 116, 123, 124, 137,
138, 140, 421, 422, 427,
429

matangazo, see *direct
statements*, 361, 427

meaning, 7, 13, 14, 15, 16,
26, 45, 48, 54, 68, 94, 97,
98, 99, 106, 117, 122,
124, 126, 141, 168, 170,
174, 192, 238, 251, 255,
273, 277, 278, 279, 280,
281, 283, 284, 286, 296,
298, 336, 344, 347, 354,
385, 387, 421, 427

**minyambuliko ya
kufanyia**, see
prepositional extension, 427

**mnyambuliko wa
kufanyika**, see *stative
extension*, 279, 427

**mnyambuliko wa
kufanyiza**, see *causative
extension*, 282, 427

mnyambuliko wa kufanyua, see *reversive extension*, 284, 427

mnyambuliko wa kufanywa, see *passive extension*, 278, 304, 427

modifiers, 342, 345, 349, 352, 353

monosyllabic verbs, 173, 183, 184, 191, 200, 204, 212, 213, 214, 215, 231, 232, 233, 234, 275, 276

mood, 3, 240, 259, 260, 261, 263, 264, 265, 266, 267, 268, 273, 275, 276, 320, 321, 366, 367, 421, 425

mtenda, see *subject*, 147, 244, 423, 427

N

na- tense, see present tense, 2, 170, 171, 172, 178

namba ya jina, see *number*, 32, 422, 428

ngeli, see *class*, 33, 34, 35, 36, 37, 38, 39, 40, 41, 276, 419, 428

nominal prefixes, 33, 34, 35, 36, 37, 38, 39, 40, 43, 152, 153, 156, 422, 426, 429

nomino ambatani, see *compound none*, 22, 428

nomino kamili, see *proper noun*, 22, 423, 428

nomino ya jamii, see *common noun*, 22, 428

nomino ya jumla, see *collective noun*, 22, 428

nomino ya pekee, see *proper noun*, 22, 428

nomino, see *noun*, 21, 22, 30, 41, 65, 150, 419, 422, 423, 427, 428, 430

number, 23, 30, 32, 41, 45, 105, 106, 117, 125, 126, 146, 320, 422, 428

nyakati, see *tenses*, 164, 424, 428

O

object markers, 3, 68, 74, 75, 100, 244, 246, 247, 251, 253, 265, 269, 270, 273, 307, 380

objects, 2, 3, 5, 15, 23, 33, 34, 35, 36, 37, 38, 39, 41, 46, 47, 49, 50, 60, 63, 64, 65, 67, 68, 71, 72, 73, 74, 75, 76, 77, 79, 81, 82, 85, 86, 89, 95, 100, 101, 102, 107, 135, 136, 139, 140, 141, 142, 145, 162, 243, 244, 246, 247, 248, 249, 250, 251, 252, 253, 255, 257, 265, 269, 270, 273, 277, 278, 281, 282, 290, 292, 303, 306, 307, 323,

327, 329, 331, 332, 335,
336, 337, 338, 341, 342,
343, 344, 349, 350, 351,
371, 378, 380, 420, 421,
422, 426, 427, 429, 431

P

part of speech, 1, 13, 16,
29, 30, 106, 315, 385,
425

participles, 3, 45, 47, 50,
191, 195, 289, 290, 291,
292, 293, 296, 297, 299,
300, 304, 344, 350, 351,
367

passive extension, 3, 277,
304, 422, 427

passive verbs, 145, 279,
303, 304, 305, 306, 329,
422, 426, 430

past tense, 7, 181, 182,
183, 185, 187, 189, 191,
209, 210, 213, 214, 216,
225, 227, 232, 233, 235,
240, 259, 261, 275, 276,
297, 299, 300, 359, 422,
430

perfect tense, 98, 100,
174, 183, 191, 192, 193,
195, 196, 198, 208, 209,
212, 216, 226, 227, 231,
235, 239, 259, 261, 280,
296, 297, 299, 300, 422,
429

phrases, 3, 4, 42, 47, 50,
51, 61, 93, 107, 108, 130,
145, 146, 150, 163, 181,
183, 219, 220, 237, 238,
240, 242, 264, 289, 290,
291, 292, 293, 301, 303,
304, 307, 319, 322, 323,
327, 328, 330, 331, 333,
341, 342, 343, 344, 346,
348, 349, 350, 351, 357,
360, 365, 371, 422, 426,
430

prepositional phrases, 3,
219, 220, 322, 323, 327,
328, 330, 331, 333, 342,
343, 349, 350

prepositions, 3, 13, 46,
47, 60, 64, 67, 68, 71, 72,
73, 74, 75, 76, 77, 91, 95,
102, 103, 124, 128, 219,
220, 221, 243, 244, 250,
251, 252, 253, 255, 278,
282, 306, 322, 323, 324,
327, 328, 329, 330, 331,
332, 333, 335, 336, 337,
338, 341, 343, 344, 350,
378, 379, 380, 422, 426,
429

present tense, 6, 47, 167,
168, 169, 170, 172, 174,
175, 177, 178, 180, 185,
192, 207, 208, 211, 212,
216, 221, 222, 225, 226,
229, 230, 234, 259, 261,
275, 280, 359, 366, 421,
422, 423, 430

pronouns, 1, 5, 13, 30, 33, 34, 36, 37, 38, 59, 60, 61, 63, 64, 65, 66, 67, 68, 71, 73, 74, 77, 78, 79, 81, 82, 87, 89, 90, 91, 92, 93, 94, 95, 96, 97, 100, 101, 102, 105, 106, 109, 113, 115, 116, 134, 145, 146, 149, 150, 173, 244, 247, 250, 255, 289, 290, 292, 327, 329, 335, 347, 348, 355, 362, 371, 386, 420, 421, 422, 426, 427, 430

proper nouns, 20, 22, 33, 38, 59, 101, 423, 428

Q

questions, 60, 71, 74, 75, 114, 131, 133, 168, 174, 181, 239, 243, 249, 250, 255, 311, 312, 331, 335, 336, 345, 346, 353, 359, 360, 361, 362, 423, 426, 430

R

reduplicated demonstratives, 386, 423, 426, 430

reduplications, 4, 385, 386, 423, 429

relative constructions, 30, 96, 97, 100, 321, 355, 423, 426, 430

S

second person, 165, 169, 170, 171, 184, 187, 188, 196, 200, 204, 213, 214, 215, 221, 230, 232, 233, 234, 422

sentences, 4, 5, 6, 13, 14, 15, 16, 20, 23, 24, 26, 27, 29, 41, 42, 46, 47, 50, 51, 54, 55, 59, 60, 61, 63, 64, 66, 69, 71, 72, 79, 81, 87, 89, 90, 92, 93, 94, 99, 100, 101, 102, 103, 105, 106, 109, 119, 122, 124, 125, 126, 128, 133, 134, 143, 145, 146, 147, 148, 149, 150, 155, 156, 161, 164, 165, 174, 175, 180, 185, 189, 198, 205, 223, 239, 243, 248, 253, 257, 263, 266, 268, 274, 290, 291, 293, 303, 304, 307, 315, 320, 324, 327, 329, 333, 338, 341, 342, 343, 345, 346, 347, 348, 349, 350, 351, 352, 353, 354, 355, 356, 357, 359, 361, 362, 365, 367, 368, 371, 380, 389, 419, 420, 423, 427, 428, 429

sentensi, see *sentence*, 348,
352, 353, 354, 419, 423,
428, 429

shamirisho yambiwa, see
indirect object, 255, 421,
429

shamirisho, see *objects*, 68,
244, 250, 255, 329, 336,
420, 421, 422, 426, 429

singular, 23, 29, 32, 33,
34, 35, 36, 37, 38, 39, 40,
41, 42, 43, 48, 63, 65, 66,
67, 72, 73, 74, 76, 81, 89,
90, 105, 106, 107, 116,
118, 121, 124, 126, 127,
132, 133, 135, 136, 146,
149, 150, 151, 155, 163,
164, 165, 169, 171, 179,
184, 188, 192, 196, 197,
200, 204, 205, 221, 264,
282, 291, 292, 295, 298,
348, 422

stative extension, 3, 277,
280, 423, 427

stems, 48, 230, 312, 313

subject prefixes, 2, 83,
85, 137, 139, 149, 150,
155, 157, 230, 291, 292,
423, 426, 429

subjunctive, 3, 240, 241,
259, 260, 261, 264, 265,
267, 268, 269, 270, 271,
272, 273, 274, 275, 321,
366, 423, 425

superlatives, 376, 377,
379, 380

synopsis, 163, 164, 165,
423, 426, 427, 429

T

tag questions, 360, 361,
423, 426, 430

tangazo, see *direct
statement*, 420, 429

tenseless relative, 99,
423, 426, 430

tenses, 2, 3, 6, 7, 8, 47, 50,
98, 99, 100, 149, 150,
151, 152, 153, 154, 161,
162, 163, 164, 167, 168,
169, 170, 171, 172, 173,
174, 175, 177, 178, 180,
181, 182, 183, 184, 185,
187, 188, 189, 191, 192,
193, 195, 196, 197, 198,
199, 200, 203, 204, 205,
207, 208, 209, 210, 211,
212, 213, 214, 215, 216,
217, 221, 222, 225, 226,
227, 228, 229, 230, 231,
232, 233, 234, 235, 237,
238, 239, 240, 242, 246,
249, 259, 260, 261, 267,
275, 276, 280, 289, 291,
295, 296, 297, 298, 299,
300, 301, 304, 305, 307,
320, 321, 322, 351, 359,
366, 372, 420, 421, 422,
423, 424, 428, 429, 430

tensi, 99, 164, 191, 196, 298, 421, 422, 423, 424, 426, 429, 430

tensi timilifu, 191, 196, 422, 429

tensi za maneno mawili, see *compound tenses*, 298, 429

third person, 126, 151, 169, 170, 171, 173, 183, 188, 192, 196, 200, 204, 205, 213, 214, 215, 221, 230, 232, 233, 234, 292, 351, 371, 422

to be, v, 2, 9, 11, 26, 31, 45, 46, 48, 53, 117, 133, 163, 168, 174, 177, 192, 196, 200, 207, 208, 209, 210, 211, 212, 213, 214, 215, 216, 219, 220, 229, 233, 238, 242, 268, 278, 279, 280, 281, 283, 284, 285, 287, 289, 292, 299, 304, 328, 331, 386, 426

to have, 2, 45, 46, 225, 226, 227, 228, 229, 231, 232, 234, 238

transitive verbs, 162, 163, 249, 423, 426, 430

two-word tenses, 298, 423, 429

U

ulinganishaji, see *comparison*, 377, 419, 429

urudufu, see *reduplication*, 385, 423, 429

V

verb extensions, 3, 277, 285, 424, 427

verb tenses, 149, 203, 259, 295, 424, 428, 429, 430

verbal nouns, 1, 40, 45, 46, 47, 48, 50, 53, 54, 55, 168, 183, 191, 200, 204, 211, 213, 232, 275, 276, 292, 424, 426, 430

verbs, v, 2, 3, 5, 6, 13, 14, 30, 45, 46, 47, 48, 50, 51, 53, 54, 63, 67, 69, 71, 73, 74, 76, 81, 83, 85, 93, 95, 98, 99, 101, 105, 106, 115, 117, 132, 137, 139, 145, 146, 147, 149, 150, 151, 152, 153, 154, 155, 156, 157, 161, 162, 163, 164, 165, 167, 168, 169, 170, 171, 172, 173, 174, 175, 177, 178, 179, 180, 181, 182, 183, 184, 187, 188, 191, 192, 193, 195, 196, 197, 198, 199, 200, 203, 204, 205, 207, 208, 209, 210, 211, 212, 213, 214, 215, 216, 219, 220, 221, 222, 225, 226, 227, 228, 229, 230, 231, 232, 233, 234, 237, 238, 240,

242, 243, 246, 249, 250,
251, 252, 253, 255, 256,
259, 261, 263, 264, 265,
267, 268, 269, 270, 272,
274, 275, 276, 277, 278,
279, 280, 281, 282, 283,
284, 285, 286, 289, 290,
291, 292, 293, 295, 296,
297, 299, 300, 303, 304,
305, 306, 307, 311, 312,
314, 315, 320, 321, 322,
323, 329, 331, 332, 335,
336, 337, 341, 342, 343,
344, 345, 346, 347, 348,
349, 350, 351, 352, 353,
354, 359, 360, 371, 372,
375, 377, 380, 385, 386,
389, 419, 421, 422, 423,
424, 426, 427, 428, 429,
430, 420

viambishi awali, see
subject prefixes, 149, 422,
423, 429

vibainishi, see *articles*, 26,
419, 429

vielezi, see *adverbs*, 312,
419, 429

vihusishi, see *prepositions*,
329, 389, 422, 429, 430

vimilikishi, see *possessive
pronouns*, 90, 123, 422,
430

vionyeshi rudufu, see
reduplicated demonstratives,
386, 430

vionyeshi, see
demonstratives, 81, 82,
136, 386, 420, 423, 430

virai, see *phrases*, 348, 422,
423, 430

virejeshi, see *relative
constructions*, 30, 96, 421,
423, 430

vishazi, see *clauses*, 348,
419, 422, 430

vitenzi elekezi, see
transitive verbs, 163, 423,
430

vitenzijina, see *verbal
nouns*, 40, 48, 420, 421,
424, 430

viunganishi, see
conjunctions, 320, 419, 430

vivumishi vya kuuliza,
see *interrogative adjectives*,
132, 430

vivumishi, see *adjectives*,
30, 116, 132, 419, 421,
422, 430

viwakilishi nomino, see
pronouns, 30, 65, 430

viwakilishi vya nguvu,
see *intensive pronouns*, 386,
430

voice, 3, 239, 303, 304

W

wakati ujao, see *future
tense*, 164, 199, 203, 420,
430

wakati uliopita, see *past
tense*, 164, 183, 187, 422,
430

**wakati uliopo
unaoendelea**, see *present
progressive tense*, 164, 169,
422, 430

wakati uliopo, see *present
tense*, 48, 150, 164, 169,
178, 421, 422, 423, 430

wakati, see *tense*, 48, 150,
164, 169, 176, 178, 183,
187, 199, 203, 312, 320,
322, 420, 421, 422, 423,
424, 430

watenda, see *subjects*, 147,
244, 423, 431

what, 8, 73, 77, 78, 87, 94,
131, 132, 133, 145, 146,
155, 157, 243, 249, 250,
252, 255, 259, 267, 307,
322, 331, 335, 336, 337,
389, 421, 422, 423

which, 7, 11, 13, 26, 29,
34, 45, 49, 54, 59, 61, 65,
69, 71, 76, 81, 82, 91, 94,
95, 96, 97, 98, 99, 100,
106, 116, 118, 122, 123,
125, 126, 128, 131, 132,
133, 134, 136, 145, 146,
149, 157, 170, 172, 174,
179, 183, 191, 196, 207,
221, 225, 229, 238, 242,
243, 246, 256, 259, 261,
263, 264, 273, 278, 279,
280, 281, 282, 283, 292,
298, 304, 306, 314, 328,

333, 335, 344, 348, 352,
355, 365, 379, 380, 385,
421, 422, 427

whose, v, 77, 94, 95, 97,
126, 131, 421

word order, 5, 331, 345,
346, 352, 353, 360, 361

ANSWER KEY

Chapter 1: INTRODUCTION TO NOUNS
1. I, date, party, calendar 2. Lulu, leg, bicycle, Dodoma 3. film, we, yesterday, me 4. woman, beauty, personality, appearance 5. Dar es Salaam, city, President

Chapter 2: ARTICLES
1. A/The student read a/the book. 2. A/The writer lives on the mainland. 3. A/The child will eat the/an orange and (the) bread.

Chapter 3: NOUN CLASS
A. 1. P 2. S 3. P 4. P 5. P 6. S 7. S or P 8. S

B. a. 7 b. 2 c. 17 d. 10 e. 5 f. 11 g. 4 h. 9 i. 6 j. 1 k. 16 or 18 l. 14

Chapter 4: VERBAL NOUNS
A. 1. to _____ (any verb) 2. to _____ (any verb) 3. to _____ (any verb) 4. to _____ (any verb) 5. to _____ (any verb)
B. 1. wanting A 2. reaching A 3. thinking VP 4. riding G 5. swimming G

Chapter 5: NEGATIVE VERBAL NOUNS
A. 1. to not walk 2. not travelling 3. not walking
B. 1. kutocheka *or* kutokucheka 2. kutokutana *or* kutokukutana 3. kutotia *or* kutokutia

Chapter 7: PERSONAL PRONOUNS
1. sisi 2. ninyi 3. wao 4. wao 5. yeye; yeye

Chapter 8: REFLEXIVE PRONOUNS
1. Anajipenda 2. Unajifahamu? 3. Alijiamini.
4. Wanajitegemea. 5. Mnaweza kujisomea?

Chapter 9: INTERROGATIVE PRONOUNS
1. what P, O 2. what A 3. whom P, O 4. whose A
5. whom P, O 6. nani P, S 7. gani A 8. gani A
9. akina nani P, S 10. nini P, O

Chapter 10: DEMONSTRATIVE PRONOUNS
1. this P 2. those A 3. these P 4. those P 5. this A 6. hii A
7. huyo P 8. yule P 9. hiki P 10. hicho A

Chapter 11: POSSESSIVE PRONOUNS
1. your A 2. yours P 3. my A 4. mine P 5. their A
6. wao A 7. wao P 8. wenu P 9. lake A 10. lake P

**Chapter 12: RELATIVE PRONOUNS/
CONSTRUCTIONS**
1. Dar es Salaam is the city to which we are going.
2. Those girls are the ones to whom I was talking.
3. This is the road on which we should be driving.
4. This umbrella is not the one with which I came.

Chapter 13: INDEFINITE PRONOUNS
1. anyone Yes 2. everyone yes 3. anyone Yes; him No 4.
him No; he No; me No; he No 5. who else Yes; you No

Chapter 15: DESCRIPTIVE ADJECTIVES
1. young A 2. short A 3. smart P 4. tall A 5. beautiful P

Chapter 16: POSSESSIVE ADJECTIVES
1. 1. yetu, we (**sisi**), car (**motokaa**) 2. zenu, you pl. (**ninyi**), cars (**motokaa**) 3. zao, they (**wao**), cars (**motokaa**) 4. yake, she (**yeye**), car (**motokaa**)
5. yangu, I (**mimi**), car (**motokaa**)
2. 1. dadake, dadaye 2. none 3. babangu 4. garile 5. pakako

Chapter 17: INTERROGATIVE ADJECTIVES
1. what → cereal; gani 2. how many → times; -ngapi 3. which → movie;-ipi 4. what → town; gani 5. what → page; gani

Chapter 18: DEMONSTRATIVE ADJECTIVES
1. this → shirt ; hii 2. that → one; ile 3. these → shoes; hivi 4. those → shoes; hivyo 5. the → hat; ile 6. hiyo → kofia 7. hapo → dukani 8. hizi → suruali 9. zile → suruali; hizi → suruali 10. hizi → suruali; hizo → suruali

Chapter 19: SUBJECTS
1. the tall trees 2. drinking tea in the morning 3. the driver 4. the storm 5. pilau

Chapter 20: SUBJECT PREFIXES
1. u(taenda) → wewe (class 1, second person singular) 2. vi(linunuliwa) → vitabu (class 8) 3. ya(nanuka) → maembe (class 6) 4. a(napenda) (class 1, third person singular) 5. wa(tagombana) → vijana (class 2, third person plural) 6. li(natupwa) → jiwe (class 5) 7. u(liuzwa) → muhogo (class 3) 8. ku(nanisikitisha) → kulia (class 15) 9. zi(tatokea) → sherehe (class 10) 10. u(naonekana) → utoto (class 14)

Chapter 21: INTRODUCTION TO VERBS & VERB TENSES

A. 1. loves V.T 2. was V.I. 3. spit V.I.; saw V.T.
    4. wants V.T.; do V.I. 5. will V.I.; be V.I.

B. present progressive: ninapenda;   simple present:
ninapenda/napenda;   present perfect: nimependa;   past:
nilipenda; future: nitapenda

Chapter 22: PRESENT

1. wanabeba   2. inahamia *or* wanahamia   3. inakua   4.
anatembelea 5. linaangalia 6. huamka 7. hufanya

Chapter 23: NEGATIVE PRESENT

A. 1. The trees are not being cut down. 2. Those houses are
    not being built. 3. I do not think of you as a nice person.
B. I don't love = sipendi; you don't love = hupendi; s/he
    doesn't love = hapendi; we don't love = hatupendi; you
    all don't love = hampendi; they don't love = hawapendi

Chapter 24: PAST

A. 1. I wanted to go to the movies. 2. The doctor was
    coming to dinner. 3. His grandmother broke her hip. 4.
    Ndizi zilipikwa. 5. Majina yao yalitajwa.
B. 1. Nilienda sokoni nikanunua machungwa.
    2. Alisema "hujambo" akaondoka. 3. You went to
    school, and then what did you do? 4. They bought
    bicycles and then travelled. 5. We cooked pilau and then
    ate.

Chapter 25: NEGATIVE PAST

1. The books were not sold yesterday. 2. The teacher did not write on the blackboard. 3. The writer did not publish a new novel. 4. Hatukuenda dukani. 5. Hakushona gauni.

Chapter 26: PERFECT

have wandered; you've said; has been grumpy; have you ever thought; have been late

Chapter 27: NEGATIVE PERFECT

1. I haven't been to that store many times. 2. We haven't had a lot of rain this month. 3. A boy has not fallen down the well. 4. Hawajaenda msikitini. 5. Baisikeli haijapotezwa. 6. Uhuru haujafika.

Chapter 28: FUTURE

you will go = utaenda; you will begin = utaanza; you will laugh = utacheka; you will walk = utatembea; you will borrow = utakopa

Chapter 29: NEGATIVE FUTURE

1. Class will not begin at 10 a.m. 2. The new store will not open next week. 3. The warm season will not be very humid this year. 4. Safari haitakwisha kesho. 5. Kitabu hakitaanguka chini. 6. Mti hautakua pole pole.

Chapter 30: THE VERB 'TO BE'

1. I am a teacher. Mimi ni mwalimu. 2. I am not a teacher. Mimi si mwalimu. 3. I have been a teacher. Mimi nimekuwa mwalimu. 4. I have not been a teacher. Mimi sijakuwa mwalimu. 5. I was a teacher. Mimi nilikuwa mwalimu. 6. I was not a teacher. Mimi sikuwa mwalimu. 7. I will be a teacher. Nitakuwa mwalimu. 8. I will not be a teacher. Sitakuwa mwalimu.

Chapter 31: THE LOCATIVE VERB 'TO BE'
1. -ko 2. -po 3. -ko 4. -po 5. -ko 6. -mo 7. -mo 8. -po 9. -po 10. –po

Chapter 32: THE VERB 'TO HAVE'
1. You have a book. Wewe una kitabu. 2. You do not have a book. Wewe huna kitabu. 3. You have had a book. Wewe umekuwa na kitabu. 4. You have not had a book. Wewe hujakuwa na kitabu. 5. You had a book. Wewe ulikuwa na kitabu. 6. You did not have a book. Wewe hukuwa na kitabu. 7. You will have a book. Wewe utakuwa na kitabu. 8. You will not have a book. Wewe hutakuwa na kitabu.

Chapter 33: AUXILIARY VERBS
was always asking; to go; had thought; buying; went; tried to buy; bargaining; was finally able to get; will ride; thought; does not need; to go

Chapter 34: OBJECTS
1. Zakia, party, town 2. donkey, market 3. dawn, family 4. books, class 5. house, party

Chapter 35: DIRECT OBJECTS
1. present 2. newspaper 3. car 4. grandmother 5. letter

Chapter 36: INDIRECT OBJECTS
1. grandmother 2. family 3. me 4. you 5. store

Chapter 38: THE IMPERATIVE MOOD
1. Children, play dominoes! 2. Students, read your books! 3. Ashur, be careful not to burn yourself while cooking!

Chapter 39: THE SUBJUNCTIVE MOOD
1. to help 2. to say 3. could come 4. be brought 5. to do

Chapter 41: VERB EXTENSIONS
A. 1. Ps. to be obstructed, blocked 2. St. to be stoppable 3. Prep. to block for/to 4. Cs. to cause to block 5. Rp. to block each other
B. 1. Ps. to be erased 2. St. to be erasable 3. Prep. to erase for 4. Cs. to cause to erase 5. Rp. to obliterate each other
C. 1. Ps. to be hit 2. St. to be strikable 3. Prep. to hit for 4. Cs. to make hit 5. Rp. to hit each other
   6. Cs. & Rp. to make hit each other

Chapter 42: PARTICIPLES
1. walking VP 2. studying A 3. learning A 4. doing VP 5. cooking VP

Chapter 43: COMPOUND TENSES
1. was walking = past progressive 2. had woken up = past perfect 3. had grown tired = past perfect 4. was wondering = past progressive 5. will I be walking = future progressive 6. will have grown dark = future perfect

Chapter 44: ACTIVE & PASSIVE VOICE
1. were moved P 2. moved A 3. was hurt P 4. hurt (herself) A 5. will sell A 6. vitauzwa P 7. aliamua kuuza A 8. aliamrishwa P 9. watanunua A 10. vitanunuliwa P

Chapter 45: ADVERBS
A. 1. beautifully → writes V 2. very → interesting Adj. 3. often → worth reading A 4. quite → sympathetic Adj. 5. extremely → sorry Adj.
B   1. Adj. 2. Adv. 3. Adj. 4. Adv. 5. Adv.

Chapter 46: CONJUNCTIONS
1. P 2. SC 3. SC 4. SC 5. SC 6. P

Chapter 47: PREPOSITIONS AND PREPOSITIONAL PHRASES
1. of Tanzania; of the mainland republic; of Tanganyika; of Zanzibar 2. by a plateau 3. in the center; of Tanzania 4. by the Great Rift Valley; of which 5. through central Tanzania; near Lake Malawi

Chapter 48: OBJECT OF THE PREPOSITION
1. the window 2. Zawadi 3. bunches 4. Swahili grammar 5. a whisper

Chapter 49: SENTENCES, PHRASES & CLAUSES
A. 1. C 2. CX 3. S 4. CX
B. 1. S 2. C 3. S 4. C 5. S

Chapter 50: DECLARATIVE & INTERROGATIVE SENTENCES
1. Does the Republic of Kenya straddle the Equator in East Africa? 2. Does Mombasa lie on the narrow coastal plane? 3. Does most of Kenya comprise high scrubland around Lake Turkana? 4. Are the Kenyan highlands in the southwest? 5. Is Mount Kenya the country's highest peak? 6. Nairobi is the capital, isn't it? 7. The Great Rift Valley cuts through western Kenya, doesn't it? 8. Mombasa is hot and humid, isn't it? 9. The coast is lined with mangrove swamps, isn't it? 10. Kenya is the world's fourth largest tea producer, isn't it? 11. Je, Kiswahili kinasemwa Tanzania? 12. Je, watu wengi wanasema

Kiswahili kama lugha ya pili? 13. Je, Waswahili wanakaa pwani ya Afrika ya Mashariki. 14. Je, wanafunzi wengi wa Kimarekani wanachagua kusoma Kiswahili?

Chapter 51: CONDITIONAL SENTENCES
1. S 2. S 3. CF 4. CF 5. S 6. CF 7. S 8. S 9. SW 10. S

Chapter 52: DIRECT & INDIRECT STATEMENTS
1. Salim told me that his ankle really hurts today. 2. I thought that made sense since he falls down all the time. 3. I said that maybe he should go to the doctor. 4. He said that he would go. 5. Salim went to the doctor who told him that he had a sprained ankle. 6. Salim aliniambia kwamba mguu wake uliumwa leo. 7. Nilifikiri kwamba haikushangaza kwa sababu anaanguka mara kwa mara. 8. Nilimwambia aende kwa daktari. 9. Alisema kwamba angeenda. 10. Salim alienda kwa daktari ambaye alimwambia kwamba alikuwa amevunja mguu wake.

Chapter 53: COMPARISIONS
1. C 2. P 3. S 4. P 5.